ROUTLEDGEFALMER
STUDIES IN HIGHER EDUCATION

Edited by
Philip G. Altbach
Monan Professor of Higher Education
Lynch School of Education, Boston College

A ROUTLEDGEFALMER SERIES

RoutledgeFalmer Studies in Higher Education
Philip G. Altbach, *General Editor*

Teaching and Learning in Diverse Classrooms

Faculty Reflections on Their Experiences and Pedagogical Practices of Teaching Diverse Populations

Carmelita Rosie Castañeda

RoutledgeFalmer

New York & London

Published in 2004 by
Routledge
29 West 35th Street
New York, NY 10001

Routledge is an imprint of the Taylor and Francis Group.

Library of Congress Cataloging-in-Publication Data

Castanĕda, Carmelita, 1960-
  Teaching and learning in diverse classrooms : faculty reflections on
their experiences and pedagogical practices of teaching diverse
populations / by Carmelita (Rosie) Castanĕda.
     p. cm. -- (RoutledgeFalmer studies in higher education)
Includes bibliographical references and index.
  ISBN 0-415-94926-2 (hardcover : alk. paper)
  1. Multicultural education--United States. 2. Educational
equalization--United States. 3. Educational surveys--United Sates. I.
Title. II. Series: RoutledgeFalmer studies in higher education
(Unnumbered)
  LC1099.3.C377 2004
   370.117--dc22   2003026485

Contents

List of Tables

List of Figure

Acknowledgments

In naming those whose guidance on the dissertation on which this book is based engenders my profound gratitude, I give foremost thanks to the faculty of my study who all shared valuable insights into their teaching practices. They generously gave of their time and knowledge to advance the understanding of teaching in diverse classrooms. They are truly exemplary teachers paving the way for the educational success of diverse students. In an era of changing demographics, these faculty are leaders in the movement to make the university a more equitable and representative institution.

My lasting thanks go to the members of my doctoral committee: Professor Pat Griffin, Social Justice Education Program and Chair of my Committee; Professor Ximena Zúñiga, Social Justice Education Program; and Professor Susan Cocalis, Department of Germanic Languages and Literature. All contributed their intellectual gifts in helping me receive my doctorate. In addition, Professor Maurianne Adams, Social Justice Education Program, expanded my knowledge of how to engage all students in the diverse classroom, and Professor Barbara Love, Social Justice Education Program, was a role model to me in my quest for greater self-actualization.

My friend, colleague, and compañero, Warren Blumenfeld, continually encouraged and supported me throughout this arduous process. I'll remember the times we shared at La Fiorentina Café having our mid-afternoon tea, meeting for our doctoral support group. His sensitivity and wisdom helped me feel both understood and motivated to continue the work that needed to be done. Warren, you paved the way for me.

I also thank Heather Hackman for teaching me the subtleties of navigating the sometimes rough seas of the dissertation journey. Sarah Zemore inspired me with her wizardlike abilities to see complexities with clarity. Joan Axelrod-Contrada was my cheerleader, always upbeat and optimistic. Madeline Peters, an amazing source of support, understands firsthand the particular challenges that I encountered. Linda Marchesani, too, helped by sharing the valuable four "C's": Crisis of choice, Crisis of commitment, Crisis of confidence, and Crisis of completion. These four C's helped me keep my process in perspective. I thank Jacqueline Price for her extraordinary way of seeing the many details. Special thanks I give to Leslie Edwards for her steadfast commitment, dedication, and talent. She was my sister in sharing the intellectual weight of this project.

My appreciation is boundless for my cherished friends, Dr. Ange DiBenedetto, Dr. Deepika Marya, Linda Kim, Sue Bell, and Mary Ray. Your ongoing encouragement helped keep me grounded and focused on completing my dissertation.

To my parents, Carmelita and Manuel Castañeda, and my extended Castañeda family, my thanks can relay only a fraction of the enrichment I feel for your continual support and for giving me a sense of who I am in the world.

Sola Deo Gloria!

Chapter 1
Introduction

> Teachers have the responsibility to recognize cultural differences and establish, within the framework of these differences, an environment that encourages all of their students. There is a concern of whether or not teachers have been adequately prepared to establish a learning environment that is fair and encouraging to students from a variety of cultural and racial backgrounds. Teachers who are ill prepared to meet these challenges may inadvertently establish differential expectations and discipline patterns that are actually discouraging and detrimental to some groups of students (Dixon, 1997, p. 69-70).

The racial, ethnic, and cultural composition of society in the United States continues to shift radically through the gateway to the twenty-first century. The President's Initiative on Race presents evidence that, "by the year 2050, people of color will make up 50% of the population [in the United States], therefore, there will not be a majority race" (April 1999). As the racial and ethnic composition of the United States grows increasingly complex, more children's lives will inevitably be informed by multiple cultures. Synchronically, our society is shifting from an aggregate of intersecting monocultures to a mosaic of coexisting multicultures within communities, families, and individuals.

College and university classrooms, as microcosms of the larger society, reflect this growing shift, which encompasses not only racial and ethnic diversity but also gender, ability, socioeconomic status, sexual orientation, language, and other social demographic groupings. Our transforming society presents a challenge to our educational systems to move away from the traditional *melting-pot* model, which advocates one homogenous, American culture through encouraging and coercing immigrant groups to abandon their cultural characteristics (Spring, 2000). The myth of the melting pot is not only hegemonic but ultimately untenable, as the White majority gives way to a plurality of cultural groups in the United States. Hodgkinson (1991) projects that by 2010 the numbers of non-White youth will have increased to 39% of the total youth population in the United States. Banks (1991) estimates that by 2020 students of color will comprise 46% of the nation's student population. Kitano points to the resulting impact upon classrooms, explaining that,

> consistent with changes in the overall fabric of U.S. society, college class-rooms reflect greater ethnic, cultural, and linguistic diversity. In addition, today's student body has a majority of women and a significant number of international students, older students, gay and lesbian students, and students with disabilities (1997a, p. 5).

In contrast to the mainly young, physically able, White male students in higher education in earlier generations, in 1991 women constituted 54.7% of students on college campuses. In Fall 1991, students over 24 years of age made up 40.8% of total nationwide enrollment, and10.5% of college students in 1992 had some form of physical and/or mental disability (Kitano, 1997a). Today, our educational systems are challenged to recognize and substantially engage with the experiences and needs of the increasingly diverse students in U.S. classrooms. Faculty members, colleges, and universities face the task of meeting students on the complicated territory of their multiple cultures.

Increasingly diverse college and university campuses may not be meeting the needs of all students in their classrooms (Schuster & Van Dyne, 1985a). As Marchesani and Adams write, "we have not yet learned how to maximize educational opportunities and minimize or remove educational barriers for large numbers of our current and future college students in our classes and institutional life" (1992, p. 10). Many educators contend that the dominant ethos in higher education continues to be decidedly White, male, and/or middle class (Diaz, 1992; Gay, 1992; Adams, 1992). Curriculum, pedagogy, and classroom dynamics at colleges and universities in the United States, whether as an overt or hidden agenda, continue to be constructed for the traditional student. The dismantling of Affirmative Action programs by a number of colleges and universities in the areas of admissions and hiring has further complicated the problem of creating an inclusive environment in the higher education classroom.

The situation facing U.S. higher education institutions is summarized by Adams, who suggests that,

> as colleges begin to examine the dominant paradigms and canons in the academic disciplines and their methods of instruction, they are inevitably struck by the motivational and learning characteristics of students who are different from the White, middle-class males who traditionally have been the dominant group in the undergraduate population. Thus, issues concerning teaching effectiveness are increasingly tied to diversity (1992, p. 19).

Moreover, Dean stresses that faculty have a responsibility to recognize the link between diverse students leaving higher education and the clash of cultures occurring in many college and university classrooms. He writes,

> with increasing cultural diversity in classrooms, teachers need to structure learning experiences that both help students write their way into the university and help teachers learn their way into student cultures. Like opponents of bilingual education, some would argue that we need to concern ourselves more with providing student access to academic culture, not spending time on student culture. But retention rates indicate that not all students are making the transition into academic culture equally well. While the causes of dropout are admittedly complex, cultural dissonance seems at the very least to play an important role (1989, p. 23-4).

STATEMENT OF THE PROBLEM

As demographics in higher education shift from monocultural to multicultural representations, many educators agree that college and university classrooms should adopt new strategies in order to meet the needs of diverse students (Adams, 1992; Anderson & Adams, 1992; Diaz, 1992; Gay, 1992; Marchesani & Adams, 1992). Adams writes that

> it seems urgent, given our new emphasis on multiculturalism, that college faculty become aware of the ways in which the traditional classroom culture excludes or constrains learning for some students and learn how to create environments that acknowledge the cultural diversity that new students bring (1992, p. 7).

Further complicating the issue is the fact that faculty in higher education often have not received formal pedagogical training; university graduate programs often work on the assumption that expertise in one's discipline is enough to meet the needs of students in one's classroom (Gaff, 1975; Kitano, 1997a; Rosensitto, 1990). In addition, many universities do not reward faculty efforts to develop or enrich their teaching practices. Often, when faculty are reviewed for tenure, teaching and service are secondary to the importance of publication (Bergquist & Phillips, 1975).

A response to the recognition of the need for pedagogical training has been the emergence of faculty development programs at colleges and universities, yet there are few faculty development and diversity training programs in the United States (Dale, 1998). One such example is the Teaching and Learning in Diverse Classroom Faculty and TA Partnership Project (TLDC Project) at the University of Massachusetts (UMASS) Amherst, which is dedicated to combining the initiative of faculty development and diversity education in the academy. The major goal of the TLDC Project was to help faculty and their teaching assistants (TAs) to provide successful, quality education to diverse groups of students. The programs that do exist are relatively new, so little is known about how programs such as the TLDC Project affect teachers' teaching and pedagogical practices in diverse classrooms (Rubino, 1994). If, as Adams writes, "all roads lead back to the faculty who have control in matters of teaching, evaluation, and curriculum," it is imperative to explore educators' teaching experiences and perceptions of their teaching practices in diverse classrooms (1992, p. 7). This research is integral to understanding teaching practices for diverse students and for supporting faculty development programs in the future.

PURPOSE OF THE STUDY

The purpose of this study is to describe how faculty who participated in the TLDC Project at UMASS Amherst reflect on their experiences and pedagogical practices as instructors in diverse classrooms.

RESEARCH QUESTIONS

The following research question guides this investigation:
    How do faculty who participated in the TLDC Project reflect on their experiences and pedagogical practices as instructors in diverse classrooms?

    Subquestions include the following:
    How do faculty think about teaching methods in a diverse classroom?
    How do faculty think about course content in a diverse classroom?
    What further support would faculty need to sustain/continue growth as educators in diverse classrooms?

SIGNIFICANCE OF THE STUDY

We are currently confronted with the realities of the quickly and radically shifting racial and cultural composition of U.S. society and educational institutions (Banks, 1991), yet there are several gaps in the literature regarding teaching in the diverse classrooms. Despite the shifts in the composition of students, faculty in higher education rarely received pedagogical training, much less training focused on cultural diversity in the classroom (Adams, 1992; Rosensitto, 1999). This study will help understand how faculty who participated in the TLDC Project developed pedagogical and curricular practices as university educators in diverse classrooms.

Further, although small numbers of faculty development programs have promoted professional and pedagogical growth for the last 30 years, there has been little assessment of the effects of faculty development programs (Dale, 1998). Faculty Development Programs that focused on teaching and learning in diverse classrooms have had only limited systematic follow-up. This study could help Faculty Development Programs know better how to support faculty teaching in diverse classrooms.

Finally, I have found only a few data-based research reports about faculty practices in diverse classrooms (Murray, 1996; Evans, 1995; Moran, 1993; Reed, 1993; McKinney, 1998). There are several studies that develop curricular models for teaching in diverse classrooms and provide personal accounts of pedagogical issues that arise in the diverse classroom (Kitano, 1997a; Adams, 1992; Adams, 1997; Ortega, José, Zúñiga, & Gutierrez, 1993; Anderson & Adams, 1992; Marchesani & Adams, 1992; Guskey, 1988; Bess, 1997; Friedman, Kolmar, Flint, and Rothenberg, 1996; Adams, Bell & Griffin, 1997). This study contributes to the limited body of literature, thus helping to develop a better understanding of how faculty think about teaching and the implementation of teaching strategies in diverse classrooms.

PERSONAL INVOLVEMENT

Teaching in diverse classrooms and helping students who have been traditionally underrepresented to bring their needs forward and achieve success in school has always been important to me. My interest in teaching and learning in diverse classrooms stems from my experiences as a woman of color, who has been both a student (primary school to graduate work) and a teacher (physical educator and fitness professional, social justice educator and staff trainer). I am a Mexican-American woman, born and raised in Sacramento, CA, and my early educational experiences occurred predominantly within private religious-affiliated schools and colleges. In those almost exclusively White-dominated institutions, aspects of cultural identity such as race, gender, ability, class, and other social groupings were not valued or addressed in the overall pedagogical practices and curriculum.

I was educated in a system that lacked Latino/a teachers who could serve as potential role models. In addition, none of my teachers had formal training to work with students of varying cultural identities. As a Mexican-American woman, I found no positive representation of my culture in textbooks. Also, I learn best in an interactive learning environment, but, at the time, the *banking method* (Freire, 1970) of education precluded bringing student experiences into the classroom. It was not until I attended a public junior college that I had faculty who helped me understand how larger societal issues impacted me (i.e., women's history). These faculty also took a personal interest in my success as a student by meeting with me outside of the classroom to help me better understand the course content. I benefited tremendously from these teachers and believe I would not be where I am today without their help and understanding. Thus, my educational background has been a major reason for my wanting to explore good teaching practices that enable all students to succeed.

Over the years, I have developed a very different educational philosophy and pedagogical model from most of the teaching styles and practices that I encountered in my past school experiences. I believe in striving for multicultural competence, which involves helping students and teachers acquire the knowledge and skills necessary for understanding and working with people from diverse cultural groups. I teach from a student-centered, multicultural, critically aware perspective. I have a personal commitment to knowing myself as an educator and knowing my students in order to facilitate an inclusive, culturally relevant environment. I am also strongly invested in inviting students to use their life experiences as text in the classroom. My conception of teaching acknowledges that the process is an art form, requiring instruction and practice. I endeavor to create an environment where students learn from each other and where I learn from the students. Together we create a complex array of communities and experiences.

I participated in the TLDC Project at UMASS Amherst. This program was beneficial in helping open my eyes to pedagogical practices that can be employed to engage students from diverse backgrounds. As a doctoral candidate in the Social Justice Education Program and as an employee trainer in the Training and Development Office at UMASS Amherst, I continue to strive toward multicultural competence in both the classroom and the workplace.

DELIMITATIONS AND LIMITATIONS OF THE STUDY

In this study, I examine selected faculty members' perceptions of their experiences and practices following participation in the TLDC Project at UMASS

Amherst. Although the findings cannot be generalized to apply to all areas of teaching in diverse classrooms, particular aspects and general themes emerging from the study may be transferable to other contexts.

Whereas the TLDC Project was designed for faculty and TAs, this study is limited to examining the faculty members who participated in the program between the academic years of 1994 through 2001. I have chosen to examine the experiences of faculty who have participated in the TLDC Project for three reasons: the teachers involved were committed to understanding and examining how to make their classrooms more successful to diverse students; the project gave participants a common framework from which to understand teaching in diverse classrooms; and my own experiences with the project provided me with valuable insights to improve my skills for working with diverse populations.

The information collected in this study emerged entirely from faculty recollections of, reflections on, and perceptions of their experiences and practices after participating in the TLDC Project; no classroom observations were involved, as the study is solely concerned with faculty's perspectives on their teaching practices. This study did not assess the TLDC Project, nor did it elicit student perspectives.

DEFINITIONS OF KEY TERMS

Assimilationist Pedagogy: teaching practices that aim at erasing important cultural differences and subsuming students' cultural groups under the overarching umbrella of the dominant cultural group. In short, hegemony as it informs education (Nieto, 2000; Spring, 2000).

Culture: "the ever-changing values, traditions, social and political relationships, and worldviews shared by a group of people bound together by a combination of factors that can include a common history, geographic location, language, social class, and/or religion. Thus, it includes not only such tangibles as foods, holidays, dress, and artistic expression but also less tangible manifestations such as communication style, attitudes, values, and family relationships" (Nieto, 1992, p. 111).

Diverse Classroom: refers to a classroom "populated by women; students of color; older, part-time, and international students; as well as students with various disabilities and a range of sexual orientations" (Marchesani & Adams, 1992, p. 9, citing WICHE, 1991; Carter & Wilson, 1991), as well as students from different linguistic backgrounds, work and class backgrounds, and so forth. Schmitz, Paul, & Greenberg write that "a multicultural classroom is much more than a collection of students who vary according to age, class, ethnicity, gender, national origin, race, religion, sexual orientation, or other variables that may, like these, be visible or invisible. The critical ingredient is a supportive learning environment fostered by a teacher who appropriately recognizes and values different cultural styles and perspectives and effectively engages students in the learning process" (1992, p. 75).

Exclusive Pedagogy: results in a course that "presents and maintains traditional, mainstream experiences and perspectives in the discipline. If alternative perspectives are included, they are selected to confirm stereotypes. The instructor conveys information in a didactic manner, and students demonstrate their acquisition of knowledge through objective or subjective written examinations. Classroom interactions are limited to question/answer discussions controlled by the instructor without attempts to support participation by all students. In the exclusive classroom, class time is not given to discussion of social issues not directly related to the discipline" (Kitano, 1997b, p.23).

Faculty Development: while there have been many definitions proffered, faculty development generally refers to initiatives directed towards "enhancing the talents, expanding the interest, improving the competence, and otherwise facilitating the professional and personal growth of faculty members, particularly in their roles as instructors" (Gaff, 1975, p. 14). Menges, Mathis, Haliburton, Marincovich, & Svinicki have defined faculty development as "the theory and practice of facilitating improved faculty performance in a variety of domains, including the intellectual, the institutional, the personal, the social, and the pedagogical" (1988, p. 291). Ebel & McKeachie have defined faculty development as "a comprehensive term that covers a wide range of activities ultimately designed to improve student learning and a less broad term that describes a purposeful attempt to help faculty members improve their competence as teachers and scholars" (1986, p. 11).

Inclusive Pedagogy: results in a course that "presents traditional views but adds alternative perspectives. Context integration in an inclusive course can range from simple addition of new viewpoints without elaboration to efforts at analyzing and understanding reasons for historical exclusion. The instructor uses a wide array of teaching methods to support students' active learning of course content. Evaluation of students occurs through several different types of assessments to ensure consideration of individual differences in expressing knowledge. The instructor monitors student participation and employs learning activities that support participation by all students" (Kitano, 1997b, p. 23).

Pedagogical Practices: the areas of pedagogical practice that this study focuses on are suggested by Marchesani & Adams: "the four dimensions of teaching and learning that appear to have particular relevance to issues of social and cultural diversity are (1) students: knowing one's students and understanding the ways that students from various social and cultural backgrounds experience the college classroom; (2) instructor: knowing oneself as a person with a prior history of academic socialization with a social and cultural background and learned beliefs; (3) course content: creating a curriculum that incorporates diverse and cultural perspectives; and (4) teaching methods: developing a broad repertoire of teaching methods to address learning styles of students from different social backgrounds more effectively" (1992, p. 11). Even though students are a component in this model, this study does not focus on student perspectives.

Social Group/Social Group Membership: refers to "a group of people bounded or defined by a social characteristic such as race, gender, religion, sexual orientation, physical or mental capacity, age, class, etc. Some social groups have relatively more social power in our society (dominants) and some have less (subordinates)" (Adams, Brigham, Dalpes, Marchesani, 1994, p. 33).

Teaching and Learning in the Diverse Classroom (TLDC) Partnership Project: a program launched at the beginning of the 1994-95 academic year at the University of Massachusetts Amherst with the primary goal of enhancing the ability of faculty and TAs to "create inclusive classroom climates" (Ouelett & Sorcinelli, 1995, p. 208). This was a year-long, funded teaching development project in which participants worked together to develop pedagogical and curricular strategies for implementing inclusive learning environments for all. The culminating experience was for each faculty and TA team to formulate a teaching project within their discipline.

Teachers' Experiences and Practices: the way that teachers think about, respond to, and implement strategies with regard to the areas of teaching methods, course content, knowledge of the self as an instructor, and knowledge of the students (Marchesani & Adams, 1992).

Transformed Pedagogy: results in a course that "challenges traditional views and assumptions; encourages new ways of thinking; and reconceptualizes the field in light of new knowledge, scholarship, and ways of knowing. The instructor restructures the classroom so that the instructor and students share power (within the limits of responsibility and reality). Methods capitalize on the experience and knowledge that students bring and encourage personal as well as academic growth. Alternatives to traditional assessment procedures are used, including self-evaluation and projects that contribute to real-life change" (Kitano, 1997b, p. 23).

CHAPTER OUTLINE

Chapter 2 details a review of the relevant literature, including the historical context of teaching in diverse classrooms in higher education, higher education as a developing multicultural organization, curriculum and pedagogical transformation, and models of teaching for diverse classrooms. Chapter 3 sets forth my research design and methodology and includes a discussion of the data collection procedures and analysis. Chapter 4 presents the survey data and analysis, as well as a discussion of the emerging themes. Chapter 5 relays analysis and discussion of the interview portion of the study, including an in-depth discussion of findings. The final chapter, Chapter 6, proffers a summary of the findings, a discussion of selected findings in relation to relevant literature, implications for future research, and concluding remarks.

Chapter 2
Review of Relevant Literature

This chapter is a review of literature relevant to contextualizing the focus of the current study, which examines the teaching practices and course content that faculty in higher education utilize in diverse classrooms. This chapter will explore the relevant literature regarding the following: the historical context for diversity in higher education, higher education as a developing multicultural organization, curriculum and pedagogical transformation, and models of teaching for diverse classrooms. The literature reviewed in this chapter is integral to understanding where higher education is in terms of serving diverse populations and to exploring how faculty, in particular, teach the increasingly diverse students in college classrooms.

As 2000 census results reveal, the racial, ethnic, and cultural composition of the United States continues to shift away from a White majority and towards a multicultural society. Along with this demographic shift in population, there has been an accompanying shift in the composition of college and university classrooms. As a recent joint report by the American Council on Education (ACE) and the American Association of University Professors (AAUP) indicates, this

> transformation ... over the past generation is unparalleled in the history of Western higher education institutions. In the early 1960s, with the exception of those attending historically black [sic] colleges and universities, only a handful of Americans of color went to college in the United States; today, upwards of one in five undergraduates at four-year schools is a minority (2000, p. 1).

The students in higher education classrooms are forming an increasingly diverse constituency (Kitano, 1997a; Adams, 1992). According to Kitano, with the exception of Native-American students, "the proportion of college enrollment comprised of diverse groups has increased steadily, while the proportion of White, non-Hispanic students has declined" (1997a, p. 5). Institutions of higher education have also witnessed regular increases in other underrepresented groups, such as women, gay and lesbian students, people with disabilities, students of non-traditional age, and international students (Kitano, 1997a).

As the diversity of college and university campuses increases, institutions of higher education have begun to identify ways in which they might transform in order to meet the needs of diverse populations. Whereas equitable access for all students has been a major concern since the 1960s, issues facing diverse campuses now also include retaining and identifying how diversity on campus may benefit all students. Essentially, as educational institutions are products of our larger culture (Asante, 1991), they reflect the major collisions that characterize that culture; thus, higher education becomes another arena in which the struggles between dominant and underrepresented groups unfold (Chesler, 1996; Chace, 1990). As Smith indicates,

> colleges and universities, pressed by both internal and external constituencies, are inevitably being called upon to clarify the larger relationship between higher education and society. Campuses of all kinds serve as a microcosm for the issues, efforts, and tensions being played out elsewhere in society (1997, p. 3).

Furthermore, there is a strong popular mandate in our society for higher education to embrace and fully address its increasingly diverse populations. According to Smith and Schonfeld, "a 1998 national opinion poll sponsored by the Ford Foundation's Campus Diversity Initiative shows that over 90% of the public believe that diversity is important and that higher education has an important role in fostering it" (2000, p. 16). Of those polled, 67% agree that "preparing people to function in a more diverse society is an important purpose of higher education" (AACU, 1999). Sixty-nine percent agree that both diversity on campus and courses and campus activities that emphasize diversity and diverse perspectives have more of a positive effect on college campuses than a negative one (AACU, 1999). As during the Civil Rights Movement of the 1950s and 1960s, social pressure is being brought to bear on institutions of higher education in order to influence change. There is great demand for universities to meet the needs of the future of organizations by addressing and supporting diversity.

In response, higher education is exploring how it might best educate and facilitate the emergence of our rapidly diversifying society. According to Smith, "there have been new efforts throughout higher education to develop a broad variety of programs and initiatives addressing access and equity, student success, campus climate, intergroup relations, curriculum, scholarship, and institutional mission" (1997, p. 3). Many educators in college and university classrooms are recognizing that students who differ demographically also differ with regard to educational needs. As Adams writes,

> as colleges begin to examine the dominant paradigms and canons in the academic disciplines and their methods of instruction, they are inevitably struck by the motivational and learning characteristics of students who are different from the White, middle-class males who traditionally have been the dominant group in the undergraduate population. Thus, issues concerning teaching effectiveness are increasingly tied to diversity (1992, p. 19).

As stated earlier, higher education has recognized areas of concern and has been actively engaged in making education more available and successful for diverse students since the social activism of the 1960s (Smith, 1997). Yet it is important to note that this is an ongoing process. Schoem, Frankel, Zúñiga, and Lewis also stress the ongoing nature of this transformation:

> today, a constructive process of reflection, debate, and exploration is occurring on many campuses; faculty members across the nation are, in a serious and scholarly manner, struggling to reshape the content and practice of their classroom teaching to expand the horizons of knowledge for all students in a way that reflects the diversity among us (1995, p. 5).

And it seems important to remember, as Smith urges, that few individuals in the United States have ever experienced a "fully pluralistic and equitable" community. Thus, higher education is learning as it goes, "innovating and changing while facing a largely unprecedented challenge" (1997, p. 3).

It is important, however, also to note that, while the recent history of higher education has been one of attempting to include those previously excluded, there is simultaneously a contemporary set of counter forces working against multiculturalism in higher education. Several contemporary theorists, including Bloom (1987), D'Souza (1991), Steele (1989), and Schlesinger (1998), question the appropriateness, rigor, and necessity of multiculturalism in higher education. The aforementioned writers have emerged out of a movement backed by the Committee for the Defense of History; but they have been criticized by multiculturalists such as Asante for being "nothing more than a futile attempt to buttress the crumbling pillars of a white [sic] supremacist system that conceals its true motives behind the cloak of American liberalism" (1991, p. 173).

According to critics such as Bloom (1987), the values of excellence and tolerance are under attack by the proponents of multiculturalism. Because of multiculturalist initiatives, these critics believe "traditionally white [sic] colleges and universities have experienced a 'revolution' that sets aside concern for excellence in favor of allegedly corrupting goals of certain racial groups, particularly African-Americans" (Feagin, Imani, & Vera, 1996, p. 2). These institutions have, in the opinion of Bloom and others, essentially become *too tolerant*. Bloom goes so far as to assert that White students on college campuses today "just do not have prejudices anymore" (1987, p. 89). Rather, these White students have helped, through their good will and open-mindedness, to create a melting-pot atmosphere that minority students simply resist and reject (Feagin, Imani, & Vera, 1996). These minority students, in Bloom's view, continue to exaggerate the existence of racism and threaten the idyllic environment of university life.

This movement against multiculturalism has important implications that must be considered if higher education is to move forward and address the needs of diverse students. Also important is the fact that the United States is, and has been since 1980, in the midst of a conservative political climate, which has had lasting effects on the development and implementation of educational change that values diversity. According to Valverde, in recent years we have witnessed attacks on affirmative action, "the core of equal opportunity," by groups such as the Christian Coalition and by legislation such as California's Proposition 209. Further, economic conditions are also having an effect on diversity in higher education. State funding to higher education continues to decline, with the result that "the poor and people of color are hit the hardest" (Valverde, 1998, p. 24).

Still, institutions of higher education and faculty members are taking up the challenges of creating pluralistic and equitable communities for several important reasons. The most basic reason is that, to continue orienting education toward the traditional White, middle-class student would be to blatantly disregard the reality of the society in which we live. Already, this kind of disregard has resulted in the fact that "our institutions of higher education are decidedly less multicultural than our society at large, not only in terms of un-diverse representations of faculty and students, but also in terms of curricular and support activities" (Chesler, 1996, p. 1). In addition, many believe that not only institutions of higher education, but also individual faculty members have moral responsibilities to transform in order to meet the needs of diverse students (Kitano, 1997a; Smith, 1997; Adams, 1992; Dean, 1989). Kitano explains that, in addition to our professional responsibility for comprehensive knowledge of the discipline, faculty members have a moral imperative to engage students intellectually and emotionally to encourage both learning and degree completion. The increasing diversity of students on our campuses coupled with disproportionately low rates of college completion by students of color demands transformation of our courses and programs (1997a, p. 3).

Beyond professional and moral imperatives for transforming higher education to meet the needs of diverse students, much evidence suggests that both the increasing diversity in higher education and multicultural transformation of courses have many benefits for students and campuses (Gurin, 1999; Smith & Schonfeld, 2000; Smith, 1997; Chang, Witt-Sandis, & Hakuta, 1999). With regard to institutions, having a "critical mass" of diverse people "create[s] greater opportunities for social support, role models, and mentoring," helps break down stereotypes, and demonstrates real commitment to diversity, which "proves important in creating an inclusive climate" (Smith, 2000, p. 18).

Additional benefits to the multicultural transformation of classrooms include improving the campus climate, heightening students' critical thinking skills, and improving intergroup relationships across campus (Gurin, 1999; Smith, 2000; Kitano, 1997a; Chang, Witt-Sandis, & Hakuta, 1999). In fact, several recent studies suggest that diversity on college and university campuses actually leads to increased learning. These studies suggest that students may attain broadened perspectives and a facility with alternative viewpoints, as well as an ability to have more complex discussions and to carry out more complex analyses (Smith, 2000). Further, research studies indicate that "student satisfaction with college and increased cultural understanding are directly related to the inclusion of multicultural material in the classroom" (Smith, Gerbick, Figueroa, Watkins, Levitan, 1997, p. 32).

The multicultural transformation of higher education in the United States affords numerous potential benefits for students from both traditional and underrepresented backgrounds, for campuses, for group relations, and for improved scholarship and intellectual integrity, besides addressing the most basic moral imperatives to meet the real educational needs of all students and move toward a more equitable society. These benefits are the driving force for educational research regarding how we might achieve such a multicultural transformation in higher education.

HISTORICAL CONTEXT FOR TEACHING IN DIVERSE CLASSROOMS

According to the late African-American leader, Marcus Garvey, "A people without a history is like a tree without roots" (Jennings, 1994, p. 14). Similarly, when investigating social and political transformation, it is important to review the historical context in which these changes arose.

This section examines the historical context in which institutions of higher education changed from predominately monocultural campuses towards integrated, multicultural campuses. Though the challenge of meeting the needs of diverse students has always been present in higher education, it is the manner of addressing this challenge that has changed over time. Higher education's history moves from exclusion toward inclusion, and it is important to think about this trajectory in order to understand the different traditions in which solutions to educational inequality have been framed. In many ways, it is difficult for educators and institutions to progress further toward inclusive education unless they are continually reflecting on past efforts.

Just as it is vital to examine the origins of higher education in order to understand the legacy of exclusion perpetuated in these institutions, it is likewise important to understand the multicultural education movement in higher education and the social-historical context out of which it arose (Sleeter & Grant, 1987; Banks, 1995; Wyngaard, 1998). Resistance to traditional pedagogy has a rich history. Noting the forms and results of this resistance are helpful in formulating new approaches to pedagogical practices and course content for diverse students.

To highlight the progression of higher education from exclusive to increasingly inclusive, I will briefly review the history of education and educational change by examining the ways in which various social groups have attempted to transform the academy. I thus examine the influence of different social groups gaining access to higher education, the influence of social movements, and curriculum transformation efforts (e.g., Ethnic Studies, Women's Studies, Disability Studies, and Queer Studies) on the academy. I will look primarily at race, ethnicity, and gender as I illustrate how higher education has responded and struggled to include diverse students. I build on the foundation of Banks's (1995) historical analysis of the lineage of multicultural education. Banks (1991, 1995) outlines four stages in the development of multicultural education: the ethnic studies movement, the multiethnic education movement, the inclusion of other underrepresented groups, and the development of theory and research.

1600-1700s: The Origins of Today's Colleges and Universities

In general, the historical trajectory of diversity in colleges and universities in the United States has progressed from exclusionary to increasingly inclusive. Harvard, the first institution of higher education in the United States, was founded in 1636. It was established for the purpose of training men to serve in the Christian clergy (Thelin, 1990). Yet, Harvard also had explicitly social and cultural goals. An early Harvard commencement speech illuminated its other objectives:

> The ruling classes would have been subjected to mechanics, cobblers, and tailors; ... the laws would not have been made by *senatus consulta*, nor would we have rights, honors, or magisterial ordinance worthy of preservation, but plebiscites, appeals to base passions, and revolutionary rumblings, if these our fathers had not founded the University ... (Thelin, 1990, p. 6-7).

Exclusion was one of the motivating factors for the founding of America's earliest institutions of higher education. These colleges institutionalized the separation among classes, genders, and people from other than Euro-Christian racial, ethnic, and cultural backgrounds.

Thelin summarized King George III's stated mission for colleges in the American colonies: "a sense of unity where, in a society created from many of the nations of Europe, there might otherwise be aimless and uncontrolled diversity. A college advances learning; it combats ignorance and barbarism" (1990, p. 13). The fear and distrust of diversity, in forms ranging from American Indians to working-class immigrants to women, made exclusion and assimilation into an Anglo-male-owning class norm integral to the fabric of American higher education during its initial formation. One example of this exclusionary and assimilationist ethic in the origins of higher education was found in colonial American attempts at instituting education for Native Americans. According to Wright,

> in many areas, the English operated under the misguided and culturally arrogant notion that education was an expedient means to Indian conversion. The resulting educational schemes were not limited to teaching the rudiments of reading writing, and catechism ... but included pompous plans for bringing higher learning ... to illiterate "savages" (1995, p. 26).

As expected from the Harvard commencement speech excerpted earlier, Harvard was one of the first institutions to initiate such an indoctrination program for male Native Americans in 1656 (Wright, 1995). These separate and unequal Indian missions, appended to traditional colonial colleges, may be viewed as a metaphor for the general trajectory of higher education in relation to minority groups throughout U.S. history — first exclusion, then a parallel program of assimilation that resulted in a failure to educate. As Wright explains, "the Indian College at Harvard, during its four decades of existence, graduated only a single Indian, and he died within a year of receiving his bachelor's degree" (1995, p. 28).

Efforts to assimilate underrepresented groups into the mainstream educational system were rare for much of the early development of higher education. In general, these institutions were exclusively for White, upper-class males. The pedagogical practices and course content that began to evolve constituted what is presently considered traditional pedagogy. Traditional pedagogy is referred to as "the old education" by the important early pioneer of educational reform, John Dewey.

Dewey (1900) advocated for abandoning certain elements of traditional education that he believed promoted passivity in students. Elements of the old education included drills, recitation, rote memorization, lecturing, total-class instruction, chalkboard exercises, and uniformity in method and curriculum. For Dewey, traditional education could

> be summed up by stating that the center of gravity is outside the child. It is in the teacher, the textbook, anywhere and everywhere you please except in the immediate instincts and activities of the child[ren themselves] (1900, p. 34).

According to Dewey, traditional education was driven by a medieval sense of the learning process and negated the potential impact that a student's own experiences could have on this process. This pedagogical approach assumed that educational "direction and control were just matters of arbitrarily putting the child in a given path and compelling him (sic) to walk there" (1900, p. 196). Interestingly, Dewey understood that traditional education was at work in higher education as well as in elementary education.

In essence, traditional pedagogy stresses academic cultural practices such as competitiveness, an emphasis on individualism, an assertive/aggressive personal presentation, knowledge acquisition, and linear styles of thinking and acting (Adams, 1992), rationality, "mastery," and the assumption of a "single universal, objective reality" (Maher & Tetreault, 1992, p. 57-8). Traditional pedagogy also includes what Freire (1970) refers to as a *banking system*, whereby an instructor deposits information into what is considered to be the student's docile, waiting mind. Adams found that, in the process, much gets overlooked and left out. Traditional pedagogy

> rules out nonverbal, empathic, visual, symbolic, or nuanced communication; it neglects the social processes by which interpersonal communication, influence, consensus, and commitment are included in problem solving; it overlooks the social environment as a source of information, together with observation and questioning as information-gathering methodologies; it ignores the values and emotions that nonacademics attach to reasons and facts (Adams, 1992, p. 6).

This form of pedagogy may be described as the natural outgrowth of Eurocentric institutions.

Thus, higher education in the United States has historically been a system in which people from marginalized groups have been compelled to assimilate. Often students who have been socialized in alternative ways "find that their values and beliefs are in conflict with many traditionally sanctioned classroom procedures that constitute an implicit or hidden curriculum" (Adams, 1992, p. 5). Ironically, there is much evidence to suggest that those who fit the model of the traditional student often do not benefit from the narrow confines of traditional pedagogy (Green, 1989). Many educators agree that, because higher education has historically been dominated by and geared toward one demographic population, where access and success are dependent upon the privilege of having been inducted into the culture of that population, these institutions "have given us at best partial truths and at worst a discourse that silences or marginalizes other ways of knowing" (Maher & Tetreault, 1992, p. 57).

1800-1930s: The Struggle to Obtain an Education

Before and during the American Civil War (1861-65), many women and African Americans began collaborating in the Abolitionist movement to end slavery in the United States (Zinn, 1980). The collaboration of these two traditionally oppressed groups initiated an examination of the ways in which their circumstances were often similar. According to Andersen, "in the nineteenth and twentieth centuries, the feminist movement emerged from the black [sic] liberation movements. In the nineteenth century ... the institutional perspective of the anti-slavery and black [sic] freedom movements influenced feminist political theory" (1985, p. 64). As education has long been viewed as one of the major routes to success and opportunity in the United States, it is no wonder that, for both women and African Americans in this period, education became a focus of their struggles.

During the post-war Reconstruction period, access to education became a primary focus for freed slaves (Zinn, 1980) and women. Yet, simultaneously, the response to the end of slavery by many institutions in both the

North and the South remained legalized segregation. As Feagin, Vera, and Imani suggested, although public education began expanding in the United States, keeping Black and White students separate became the answer to maintaining a "racial caste system" (1996, p. 10). As a result, the admission of African-American students to historically White colleges and universities was rare: "from 1826, when the first Black American graduated from Bowdoin College, to 1890, only thirty Black Americans graduated" from these institutions in the United States (Feagin, Vera, & Imani, 1996, p. 10). Even by 1910, the number remained under 700. It wasn't until the 1960s that African Americans in the United States were admitted in significant numbers to historically White institutions (Feagin, Imani, & Vera, 1996).

One response to the exclusion from traditional colleges and universities was the establishment of separate institutions. The first women's college, Mt. Holyoke, was established in 1837. Soon other women's colleges were founded, such as Vassar in 1865, Smith College in 1872, Wellesley College in 1875, and Bryn Mawr in 1886. Women's colleges continued to proliferate throughout the nineteenth century. According to Faderman, "by 1880, forty thousand women, over a third of the higher education student population in America, were enrolled in colleges and universities and there were 153 American colleges that they could attend" (1991, p. 13). There were, however, many conservative critics who attacked this new trend, warning that educated women would be unfit to fill traditional roles in society. Others, such as Dr. Edward Clarke in 1873, warned that studying those subjects that men studied would interfere with women's fertility, causing them chronic uterine disease (Faderman, 1991).

With regard to African Americans, Wyngaard states that "between 1868 and 1898, 30,000 Black teachers were trained" and Black universities such as "Howard [1866], Tuskegee [1881], Fisk [1866], Hampton [1912], and Spelman [1881] were created and thrived" (1998, p. 15).

Simply having separate institutions was often not sufficient to remedy past inequalities. Integral to ensuring that women's colleges and Black colleges provided real educational opportunities was guaranteeing that they were not reproducing traditional oppressive and exclusionary pedagogies and curriculum. This, however, was a significant problem. Before the 1830s, women's schools were simply assimilating students into the role of "domestic scientists" by instructing women in those skills traditionally designated as gender appropriate (Faderman, 1999). Likewise, according to Feagin, Imani, and Vera, "even the segregated black [sic] ... colleges and universities were not under the full control of black educators.... [They] were created and run in a white-oriented [sic] framework that downplayed the contributions of African and African-American cultures" (1996, p. 11).

A few women's colleges during the 1920s to1960s avoided both demeaning lessons in homemaking that served to reinforce women's traditional social roles and the simple transposition of traditional pedagogy onto a separate institution for women. In general, however, these were the two models that dominated (Elliot, 1985). According to Faderman,

> although these [women's] colleges were generally interested in "elite" young women — that is, those of the middle and upper classes and of white [sic] Anglo-Saxon Protestant parentage — the move to educate women soon affected a broader spectrum (1991, p. 180).

Stemming from the success and visibility of historical women's colleges and Black colleges, the struggle for educational equity led to the early Ethnic Studies (ES) movement during the late nineteenth and early twentieth centuries. This movement advocated for the inclusion of new departments within traditional institutions of higher education. The early ES movement was exemplified in the work of scholars such as Williams (1882), Woodson (1933), and DuBois (1935), who were concerned about the ill effects that assimilationist education might have on African-American children (Banks, 1991). These scholars were integral to "creating scholarship in Ethnic Studies and teaching materials, which were integrated into the Black schools and college curriculum" (Wyngaard, 1998, p. 16). According to Banks (1995), this early part of the ES movement constituted the first phase of the multicultural education movement, which, in turn, is the basis for much of the literature reviewed in this chapter.

1940s-1950s: Attempts at Racial Harmony without Social Justice

The ES movement became less prominent as the "intergroup" education movement arose. The Intergroup Education (IE) movement grew out of the social unrest that characterized the post—World War II era in the United States. The "Great Migration" of African Americans looking for employment in the North during and following the war years and the influx of Mexicans in the West resulted in intense racial and ethnic tension over economic issues between people of color and European Americans. The response in education was the IE movement, which sought to "help reduce prejudice and create interracial understanding among students from diverse national, religious, and racial groups" (Taba & Wilson, quoted in Banks, 1995, p. 8). This movement was not concerned with addressing the institutionalized nature of "racism, power, and structural inequity," according to Banks (1995, p. 9), focusing instead on racial and religious harmony.

At the same moment as the genesis of the IE movement, some new faces were entering higher education after WW II. Land-grant institutions such as UMASS Amherst, charged with the responsibility of public education, were flooded with an influx of predominantly working-class, White, male students coming to college on the G. I. Bill of Rights. Many of these students would never have gained entrance to higher education without this program of government subsidy and mandate directed toward successfully reintegrating soldiers into the postwar economy. In fact, the nationally funded G. I. Bill is what Brodkin terms "affirmative action" for primarily males:

> The G. I. Bill of Rights, as *The 1944 service man's readjustment act* was known, is arguably the most massive affirmative action program in American history.... I call it affirmative action because it was aimed at and disproportionately helped male, Euro-origin GIs.... [Benefits] were decidedly not extended to African Americans or to women of any race. Theoretically they were available to all veterans; in practice women and Black veterans did not get anywhere near their share (1998, p.38, 42).

Whereas the early ES movement sought to promote and fight for the African-American community, the IE movement "promoted a weak form of diversity and the notion that "we are different but the same" (Banks, 1995, p. 9). According to Banks, the IE movement was an important precursor to the Civil Rights Movement and the second wave of Ethnic Studies. Further, Banks stated that IE was linked to the contemporary multicultural education movement because it shared many of the goals of today's multicultural education movement, and it experienced many of the same problems (Banks, 1994; Taba & Wilson, 1946, cited in Banks, 1995). IE's attempts to promote interracial harmony and reduce tension by proposing "concepts and understandings about groups and relations, sensitivity, and good will objective thinking, and experiences in democratic procedures" (Taba & Wilson, 1946, cited in Banks, 1995, p. 9). Later, the Civil Rights Movement did not use these IE strategies to promote its vision of change. The Civil Rights Movement advanced the notion of Ethnic Studies that Banks describes as the second phase in multicultural education: Multiethnic Studies.

1950s-1960s: The Civil Rights Movement and Demands for Equity in Education

The Civil Rights Movement and the Women's Movement in the United States resisted racism, sexism, and exclusionary institutions. Importantly, the legality of separate-but-equal education was overturned by the Supreme Court in the case of *Brown v. Board of Education*. Although many areas of public life remained segregated for years to come, it was during this period that historically White institutions were mandated to admit significant numbers of African-American students (Feagin, Imani, & Vera, 1996).

The ES Movement resumed full-force during the Civil Rights Movement in the 1950s. The goals of ES were to include all students — those of color, White, majority, and underrepresented ethnic identities (Suzuki, 1979) — to help students to "view events, concepts, issues, and problems from diverse cultural and ethnic perspectives" (Banks, 1991, p. 3), to "develop cross-cultural competency, which consists of the abilities, attitudes, and understandings students need to function effectively within the American national culture, within their own ethnic subsocieties, and within and across different subsocieties and cultures" (p. 9), and to develop "decision-making and social action skills" (p. 24).

Although the doors of higher education were opening to increasing numbers of formerly underrepresented students, the organizational structures of these institutions remained virtually the same. For instance, according to Feagin, Imani, and Vera,

> even in 1960, there were no more than two hundred black [sic] faculty members in traditionally white [sic] colleges and universities. Most traditionally white Northern and Southern universities had very few black faculty members until the 1970s. Even today, most of the nation's predominantly white colleges and universities have only token numbers of African American faculty members (1996, p. 11).

Further, people of color accounted "for only 12.9% of full-time faculty and 9.6% of full professors in 1995" (Mellander, citing the ACE Report, 1998, p. 15).

As groups of students who had been previously excluded from higher education began to fill college classrooms, those both within the academy and from the larger society began to question the quality of teaching. Gaff revealed that, during the 1960s, faculty in higher education came under intense fire for "irrelevant courses, uninspired teaching, and impersonal relationships with students" (1975, p. 15). It became clear to many involved in higher education that simply opening the doors to previously excluded groups would not be enough. Instead, a process of comprehensive transformation needed to occur.

According to Banks, it was at this point that

> educators interested in ethnic studies began to realize that inserting eth-
> nic studies content into the school ... was necessary but not sufficient to
> bring about school reform that would respond to the unique needs of
> ethnic minority students and help all students to develop more demo-
> cratic racial and ethnic attitudes (1995, p.10).

Thus, progress toward *multi*ethnic education ensued, which was oriented
toward increasing educational equality through "structural and systemic
changes" (1995, p. 10). This, in Banks's view, constituted the second phase
in multicultural education.

1960s-1970s: Underrepresented Groups Demand Equal Representation and Treatment in Addition to Equal Access

As mentioned earlier, once such underrepresented groups as women, people
of color, and people with disabilities began entering U.S. colleges and universities, they often found that the traditional curriculum neither represented their experiences nor addressed their needs. In essence, traditional
pedagogy and course content, which developed with White, middle-class,
male, and predominately Christian students in mind, was often incongruent
and incompatible with the needs of students from other backgrounds. According to Banks, this period, when multiple underrepresented groups began
to work toward their inclusion in the curriculum, was the third phase of
multicultural education, which was marked by the fact that

> other groups who viewed themselves as victims of the society and the
> schools, such as women and people with disabilities, demanded the in-
> corporation of their histories, cultures, and voices into the curricula and
> structure of the schools, colleges and universities (1995, p. 10-11).

During this period, group studies programs such as Women's Studies, Black
Studies, and Asian Studies began to grow within the confines of higher education. Perceiving the profound absence or marginalization of their subjects,
these programs were the first to initiate curricular transformation in colleges
and universities. Schuster and Van Dyne described this process of filling in
the gaps:

> Our advances in transforming traditional curriculum began in women's
> studies with a process of negative definition: we identified what is need-
> ed by cataloging what was missing or marginalized. Reimagining the
> core of the liberal arts curriculum, then, means exposing the conflict be-
> tween opposing worldviews: an exclusive, white [sic], male, Western Eu-
> ropean view of human experience that calls itself humanist, in contrast

to a much more inclusive vision of critical differences in gender, ethnicity, and socio-economic backgrounds (1985c, p. 162).

The group studies approach from the 1970s to the present has thus been based in a fundamental critique of the exclusive and one-sided nature of the higher education curriculum. According to Andersen, "each [group studies program] rests essentially on the premise that the experience of traditionally excluded groups has been denied, ignored, and undercut by traditional knowledge; thus reconstruction of the curriculum begins through developing a more pluralistic body of knowledge" (1985, p. 63-64).

The message sent by group studies programs and curricular change efforts in many ways goes to the heart of the major goal of the multicultural education movement. If, as Wyngaard summarizes, "schooling is affected by race, class, and gender and therefore Eurocentric curriculum is inappropriate and mis-educates all students," then, as multicultural educators and scholars have suggested, it becomes necessary to acknowledge that "schooling should reflect multiple viewpoints grounded in the variety of experiences of people" (1998, p. 23). Investigating ways to transform curriculum and examining the ways in which knowledge is constructed and delivered across all disciplines in higher education became the contemporary focus of multicultural education. This, then, is the fourth phase of multicultural education as identified by Banks: "this phase consists of the development of theory, research, and practice that interrelate variables connected to race, class, and gender" (1995, p.11). This developing body of theory and research is vital to institutionalizing transformation in higher education and in constructing a framework within which people at all levels of the institution may work.

So we have reached our current position — Banks's (1995) fourth phase of multiculturalism — by a somewhat circuitous trajectory, beginning in colonial America with the history of the Native-American presence in institutions such as Harvard University. By the mid- to late-nineteenth century there emerged separate institutions of higher education for Black people and for women. From this emanated the first phase of ES that was incorporated within Black colleges and then integrated into more traditional institutions. At that time, ES entered a hibernation period, to reawaken later. We then entered a period of the IE movement, which immediately proceeded the birth of the Civil Rights Movement. The Civil Rights Movement was a call for equal rights and opportunities for many previously underrepresented groups. In turn, the commitment of the Civil Rights Movement to equality for many underrepresented groups resuscitated the previous ES movement and expanded its scope to include addressing multiple perspectives and critically examining educational and societal disenfranchisement.

HIGHER EDUCATION AS A DEVELOPING MULTICULTURAL ORGANIZATION

As it was important to examine the historical context that has shaped contemporary institutions of higher education, it is likewise necessary to investigate the very nature of change as it relates to all levels of higher education to assess where we have been and to help map the path toward truly developing inclusive systems of education. In the following section, I use Multicultural Organizational Development (MCOD) as a theoretical lens through which I look at organizational change in higher education. I have chosen MCOD because it specifically details the process by which organizations can and do meet the needs of a diverse population. It is clear that transforming an organization requires that change take place on different levels and in different spheres (Kitano, 1997a; Valverde, 1998; Chesler & Crowfoot, 1989, 1997; Beckhard & Pritchard, 1992; Schultz, 1992). To understand how higher education may progress from monoculturalism to multiculturalism, we must first address the nature of transformation and change. Preliminary to this discussion we must first look at the definition of an organization.

Institutions of higher education fit Daft's definition of organizations as "social entities that are goal-directed, deliberately structured activity systems with a permeable boundary" (1995, p. 10). By social entities, Daft refers to the people and groups of people who comprise organizations. These organizations are goal-directed in that they are founded and exist for a single or multiple given purposes. Organizations are "deliberately structured activity systems" in that they "perform work activities." Membership is "distinct, and there are boundaries determining who and what is inside or outside the organization." Daft contends, however, that these boundaries can be permeable and not necessarily rigid because many organizations "share information and technology to their mutual advantage" (p. 10). Institutions of higher education certainty fall well within the definition of organization.

Models of organizational change often have parallel implications for educational institutions (Chesler & Crowfoot, 1997; Obear 1993, as adapted from Jackson & Holvino, 1988; Valverde, 1998). According to Chesler and Crowfoot, mission, culture, power, structure, and resources are five elements "basic to all organizations" (1989, p. 16):

Mission

- Statement of goals and purposes
- Vision of the future
- Source of legitimacy for status quo or for change
- Relates organizational goals to broader society
- Includes multiple or conflicting goals or subunits
- Relatively not open to debate
- Official (manifest) or unofficial (latent) purposes

Culture

- Dominant belief systems reflected in values, rituals, technology, styles and customs
- Norms for "proper" behavior and criteria for success
- Degree of monoculturalism or pluralism of the approved culture
- Standard for the allocation of rewards and sanctions
- Includes alternative (complementary or conflicting) cultures based on age, gender, race, class, and the like
- May include procedures for negotiating dominant and alternative cultures "Rules of the game"
- Belief system justifying basic organizational tasks and procedures

Power

- Formal decision-making hierarchies and procedures
- Degree to which access to power hierarchy is closed or open
- Constituencies that influence power-holders
- Degree of grass roots participation in key decisions
- Procedures for dealing with alternative power bases, formal (unions) and informal
- Decentralized unit control

Structure

- Division of labor among units and subunits, and related roles
- Technology for achieving organizational goals (pedagogy)
- Networks of social interaction and communication
- Planned activities that help accomplish basic tasks
- Boundary systems mediating organization's relationship with the external social and physical world
- Procedures used to achieve goals

Resources

- Materials required to accomplish organization's goals
- People
- Money
- Plant and facilities
- Raw materials and markets
- Information (Chesler & Crowfoot, 1989, p. 14)

Based upon this framework, I understand universities to be organizations; mission, culture, power, structure, and resources are core, defining aspects of higher education institutions. The status of universities as organizations becomes increasingly clear when the general place of organizations in U.S. culture is established; Daft writes that

> organizations are not just all around us; they are the prominent social institution of our time. Charles Perrow proposed that organizations are the key phenomenon in existence today ... large organizations have changed politics, because politicians come from organizations and are beholden to them. Social class is determined by rank and position within organizations, not vice versa. The family has been shaped to cope with the organizational phenomenon, with most families being dependent on organizations for wages and livelihood. Religion has even become a large organization phenomenon (1995, p. 11).

It quickly becomes apparent that many institutions embedded in our social fabric are organizations that operate according to certain principles, function in particular ways, have influence over people and communities, and likewise engender potential problems.

Like all organizations, institutions of higher education are political entities that promote and sustain particular value systems (Chesler & Crowfoot, 1989; Asante, 1991; Schultz, 1992). These organizations carry their own history of struggling to achieve equity and inclusiveness among diverse individuals in areas such as the university mission, administration, technology, faculty, students, and campus climate. Viable, comprehensive, long-term multicultural change in education will need to address the multiple layers and elements that perpetuate exclusion (Hardiman & Jackson, 1994; Chesler, 1996; Beckhard & Pritchard, 1992). The implication for fundamental change is that *all parts and aspects* of an organization such as higher education will change (Beckhard & Pritchard, 1992). Like other organizations, higher education has implemented and experienced change on multiple levels because of executive, legislative, and judicial mandates such as Affirmative Action and the direct influence of diverse populations involved in popular social movements such as the Civil Rights Movement, the Women's Movement, the Gay/Lesbian/Bisexual/Transgender Movements, and the Disability Rights Movement.

In the end, the goal is to transform higher education into a fully multicultural organization. But, as Chesler and Crowfoot indicate, many of us have never experienced the realities that this concept entails:

> We realize that few or no higher education organizations (or organizations in any other sphere of U.S. life) can claim currently to be fully (or nearly) multicultural; the best we see are systems struggling with the transition to more just states of affairs. And these transitions are by no means linear or universal; development may be unbalanced across these different organizational components and the process of struggle may progress and regress over time. In all likelihood our definitions and indicators of multiculturalism will change as we approach that stage of development — as we get closer we will see this vision more clearly (1997, p. 3).

Therefore, it is important to articulate the major aspects of the multicultural vision for higher education. Obear provides a concrete proposal regarding the elements that a truly multicultural campus should include:

1. An environment where all students can learn and contribute to the best of their abilities. An environment in which educational opportunities are maximized for all and where barriers and obstacles to this are interrupted, eliminated or minimized.
2. An environment where role models teach the skills, knowledge, and personal awareness competencies students will need to live and work effectively in a pluralistic society and world.
3. A community that models the vision and values of multiculturalism: including, but not limited to inclusion, empowerment, visibility, equity, access, social justice and shared responsibility and leadership (1993, as adapted from Jackson & Holvino, 1988, p. 1).

Obear (1993, as adapted from Jackson & Holvino, 1988) provides an important vision of what a transformed campus might include in the future. Yet the focus currently needs to be on initiating this transformative process.

Further, Obear (1993, as adapted from Jackson & Holvino, 1988) and Valverde (1998) describe a coherent, gradual process by which a university might begin to approach this vision of comprehensive, multicultural change. As mentioned previously, higher education institutions are organizations, and, in order for comprehensive change to take root, it must address the

Table 1 Models of Multicultural Transformation of Higher Education Campuses

Author	Stages 1	2	3	4	5	6
Valverde, L. (1998)	Monocultural Campus / Devoid of minority traits	Ethnocentric Campus / Dominant White culture, which admits minority	Accommodating Campus / Personnel and policies modified to accommodate people of color	Transitional Campus / Limited pluralism	Transformed Campus / Multicultural in all aspects	
Obear, K. (1993)	The Exclusionary Organization / Intentionally restricts membership	The Club / Entrance limited and monocultural norms view as "correct" way	Compliance / Commits to access and no change in policies, procedures, etc.	Affirmative Action / Actively hires, recruits and provides support for underrepresented members	Redefining Organization / Critically questions organizational structures and actively strives to become a multicultural organization	Multicultural Organization / Values contributions from all groups and committed to eliminating oppression

multiple levels and aspects of the organization. Change in this context must be viewed in a process-oriented fashion to accommodate the complex inter-relationships of levels and aspects of the organization (Jackson & Holvino, 1988). As Valverde expresses, change at universities will be slow and will al-most certainly progress episodically. The available research indicates that "it takes approximately 50 years for an innovation to be institutionalized in an educational agency" (1998, p. 25). Further, Valverde writes,

> using the last 35 years (since 1963) to frame the discussion of the grad-ual inclusion of multiculturalism in higher education institutions and to measure the progress of diversifying post-secondary campuses, reported statistics reveal an up-and-down trend (1998, p. 19, citing Carter & Wilson, 1992).

Both Valverde (1998) and Obear (1993, as adapted from Jackson & Holvi-no, 1988) discuss change for universities bearing several important issues in mind. Both address multicultural transformations in higher education as a multidimensional process (see Table 1). Both models are fairly similar and demonstrate the gradual progression of higher education from total exclu-sivity, to varying degrees of accessibility and acceptance, to complete trans-formation, plurality, and ongoing critical examination of organizational elements. Both models are also useful in understanding the process of change as it might be experienced by an organization.

Valverde (1998) compiled a five-stage developmental model charting the process from a monocultural campus to a transformed campus. At the near end of his multicultural transformation model is his first stage or "Monoc-ultural Campus" emphasized by an exclusion of underrepresented popula-tions. The second stage of his model is the "Ethnocentric Campus," which is a campus that admits underrepresented groups when and if they conform to the dominant cultural paradigm. Stage three in this model, the "Accom-modating Campus," includes those campuses that modify their policies to accommodate people of color — a way of adding on to an existing paradigm without any underlying systemwide changes. Stage four, the "Transitional Campus," begins to make some system changes and incorporates limited pluralistic notions. The fifth and final stage, the "Transformed Campus," fully integrates multiculturalism throughout all aspects of the institution.

In comparison, Obear's (1993, as adapted from Jackson & Holvino, 1988) developmental model of multicultural campus transformation is a slightly more detailed model involving six stages. Her first stage, "the Exclu-sionary Organization," is in some ways similar to Valverde's first stage, "Monocultural Campus," but goes further in that it intentionally restricts membership of various groups. Obear's stage two, "The Club," is virtually the same as Valverde's "Ethnocentric Campus," in that it limits entrance of traditionally underrepresented groups to those who can assimilate into the dominant cultural paradigm. Stage three, "Compliance," welcomes members from varying cultural groups to enter the institution while making no institutional commitments to undertaking systematic change. Obear's next two stages, stages four and five, are very similar to Valverde's stage four, the "Transitional Campus." In Obear's stage four, the "Affirmative Action" stage, the institution actively hires, recruits, and provides support for underrepresented members. In stage five, the "Redefining Organization," organizational structures are critically questioned, and the organization actively strives to become more multicultural. In Obear's final stage, the "Multicultural Organization" (the equivalent of Valverde's stage five, the "Transformed Campus"), the organization values the contributions of all groups. Obear goes beyond Valverde's final stage in that she adds the commitment of the organizations to elimination of oppression.

It is interesting to note that, in the current historical moment, institutions of higher education would be at varying stages if we were to chart them on one or both of the above developmental models. Valverde (1998) asserted that there are few fully multicultural or pluralistic higher education campuses. As with any movement that aims to make change progressively in order to include those who have been disenfranchised and marginalized, the multicultural education movement in the United States has been under attack since the Reagan Presidency (Schultz, 1992). Although this is a reactionary response, it is important to examine the available critiques and engage the questions raised in those critiques. Schultz analyzes the following eight arguments that are often raised against multicultural education:

1. **Multiculturalism views ethnicity as destiny:** focusing on larger group identities destroys the Western view that the individual is supreme.
2. **Multiculturalism sacrifices truth:** if we look at knowledge in terms of being constructed in relation to power and culture, then we lose objectivity and the "right" answer.
3. **Multiculturalism results in a sacrifice of standards:** equal representation by necessity means lowering and abolishing standards.
4. **Multiculturalism loses what is central to Western culture:** we will lose Shakespeare and Milton if we allow other kinds of texts and voices into our canon, and so on.
5. **Multiculturalism is relativism:** with multiple perspectives, there will be no way to critique or evaluate.

6. **Multiculturalism is the New McCarthyism**: multiculturalism is about being politically correct and restricts what can be said.
7. **Multiculturalism threatens a loss of power and prestige to currently powerful elites**: more egalitarian social and cultural relationships will undermine the power certain people experience.
8. **Multiculturalism destroys community**: with emphasis on group identity comes a provincial separatism (1992, p. 24).

Schultz (1992) responds to critics of multiculturalism by pointing out that their arguments are often vague and inflammatory and lack grounding in historical realities. Further Schultz contends that the "core themes within the criticisms ... suggest that the anti-multiculturalism argument is rooted in an ideology of assimilation which denies or seeks to obliterate differences among groups" (1992, p. 23). She stresses that the arguments outlined above do not rise out of a vacuum but are part of a coherent ideological position put forward by politically conservative and reactionary individuals, groups, and movements.

Schultz (1992) addresses anti-multiculturalism arguments with the following points about the realities of multiculturalism, its purposes and goals. First, multiculturalism is not *against* individuality, but rather *for* the complexity of individuals and the recognition that diverse identities provide opportunities for individuals to grow. Multiculturalism supports the development of structures and processes that facilitate communication and understanding across group boundaries and among individuals. Second, proponents of multiculturalism propose that, because knowledge is constructed, it is therefore subjective; thus, multiculturalism seeks a more balanced contribution from diverse groups toward the construction of knowledge. Third, multiculturalism seeks, not to abandon standards, but instead to critically examine traditional standards and their legitimizing sources, particularly in light of other groups' standards and values. Fourth, multiculturalism calls for the enriching of Western culture by positioning it within the context of other world cultures, rather than the complete destruction of Western culture. Fifth, unlike McCarthyism, multiculturalism seeks open access for all, not the perpetuation of silence, oppression, and exclusion. Sixth, multiculturalism endeavors to break down ethnocentric boundaries that inhibit community building. Finally, while it *is* valid to argue that multiculturalism would alter the power and prestige held by social and cultural elites, it would be more appropriate to point out that multiculturalism simply advocates that all people experience empowerment. Power would therefore be shared more equitably.

It seems clear that, for real and lasting multicultural transformation to occur in higher education, the movements antagonistic to multiculturalism need to be acknowledged and confronted, and those who advocate for multicultural education must work on multiple levels to enact change. As Valverde (1998) reminds us, external forces, like large social movements, cannot be the only factors involved in change. They stress that additionally, internal pressure, such as that generated by faculty and students, is necessary to make long-term, comprehensive change. Valverde suggests that faculty play one of the more influential roles in this transformation process and that students have a relatively low level of participation. Whereas I agree about the large responsibility of faculty, I would stress the vital role that students have played in advocating for inclusion and change on university campuses (Zinn, 1980). For example, students have been key to the movement for institutional change since at least the early 1960s and continuing in various degrees to the present day. Still, it is true that, increasingly, faculty, staff, and students need to have, and are having, an increasing effect on change at colleges and universities (Valverde, 1998). This kind of internal change effort will be one of the only ways to move campuses from accommodation or compliance, which is change motivated and instituted by external forces, such as public funding sources and social movements.

This idea is clearly echoed when Valverde states that during the last two decades there has been a significant shift in goals and strategies with regard to transforming higher education campuses and diversity. No longer is the goal of access enough. The next step is to "change a traditionally homogenous white [sic] institution into one that [is] heterogeneous or at least less racist" (1998, p. 21). Movement toward a more pluralistic, multicultural environment in higher education has become the new locus of struggle. Valverde, as previously mentioned, and Adams (1992) see faculty playing a potentially large role in influencing change. According to these authors, faculty do have a large responsibility in the areas of curriculum and pedagogical practice for diverse classrooms, and there are many ways in which faculty might begin to influence multicultural change, including curricular and pedagogical transformation.

As I have shown, Multicultural Organizational Development models are useful in understanding, examining, and evaluating the changes that have occurred, as well as the changes that need to take place if we are going to transform our institutions of higher education to truly reflect diverse populations. Redefining the mission, culture, and organizational structure of higher education would require orderly and evolutionary change. One critical dimension of change concerns curriculum and pedagogical transformation.

CURRICULUM TRANSFORMATION

Transformation of curriculum and the ways in which knowledge is constructed and legitimized are central to the goals and philosophy of multicultural education (Wyngaard, 1998). As the substance of what gets taught in higher education, curriculum is an important place to begin when examining the ways in which faculty might be involved in the process of moving education in a multicultural direction.

Curriculum can be defined in many ways, but most definitions include the notion that curriculum is a comprehensive set of complex relationships between multiple variables regarding the task of instruction (Gay, 1995). Gay defined curriculum as a "substantive phenomena," distinguished by "goals, objectives, activities, and evaluation, intended outcomes and subject matter, and the scope and sequence of instruction," as a "system," as well as "an area of professional scholarship and research" (1995, p. 27). Ayers likewise defined curriculum according to its system of complex relationships, as

> a dynamic process that is the sum total of what is taught and learned throughout the school experience. It is more than books and lesson plans — it is relationships, interactions, feelings, and attitudes. The curriculum reflects our values as teachers, parents, and communities, so we must become explicit about large goals and overriding purposes. For me, deep thinking, equity, and multiculturalism are critical, even at the earliest levels (1995, p. 18).

Additionally, Ayers (1995) expressed the process-orientation of curriculum.

Finally, Kindsvatter, Wilen, and Ishler defined curriculum using broad strokes: "one must plan to teach *something* for some *purpose*" (1996, p. 104). Both the "something" and the "purpose" comprise the curriculum. Most important, however, to Kindsvatter, Wilen, and Ishler is the "purpose" aspect of the definition (p. 104-5). This can vary from a linear, beginning-to-end process of learning course material, to incorporating all the experiences students absorb under the teacher's guidance, to a liberatory approach that stresses discovering the curriculum among the students rather than imposing one (Wiles & Bondi, 1993; Caswell & Campbell, 1935; Eisner, 1990).

In particular, I believe that curriculum is a process, including many variables, and necessarily dependent upon, as well as reflecting, the pedagogical practices and educational philosophies of educators. The three models above — the first highly theoretical, the second approaching curriculum from a more relational focus, and the third, taking a process-orientated focus — taken together adequately express my overall understanding of the term *curriculum*.

What follows is an examination of what it would mean to change or transform curriculum in order to move classrooms in higher education away from a monocultural model and towards an inclusive, multicultural model. Further, the following section examines those aspects of higher education curriculum that might be transformed and presents various conceptions of what might constitute a curriculum as it progresses through the process of transformation. In particular, the following section focuses on the components of course content and instructional strategies within the scope of curriculum in general. I contend that teachers have the most immediate and direct control over these aspects of higher education curriculum, and thus research exploring the relationship between teachers and their diverse classrooms would benefit most by concentrating on the aspects of course content and instructional strategy.

Examining how educators might transform curricula in colleges and universities with the goal of multicultural education initially begins with a contemplation of why change is necessary and with a vision of the change process. As previously noted, the history of higher education in the United States has been based on the exclusion of many underrepresented groups. As a microcosm of our society, higher education has reinforced and perpetuated inequities. A curriculum that attempts to transform higher education in order to establish inclusion for all by necessity needs to be informed by this history and the powerful obstacles to change that it represents. As Butler and Walter stress,

> the academic and social change envisioned through transformation will not come easily. We are only beginning to undo the effects of the distortion and inequities set in motion 500 years ago when Columbus brought massacre and the most brutal form of slavery known to these shores, all in the interest of spreading "Western Civilization" with all its long lasting assumptions of racial, cultural and male superiority. The praxis must be pursued with a constant, eager patience that has as its reward, in our lifetime, the concrete beginnings of change for the better for all (1991, p. 325).

Historically, a few faculty members within individual courses, departments, or programs have enacted curriculum change process in higher education in a piecemeal fashion. But the comprehensive history of oppression and exclusion demands that curricular transformation must occur on multiple levels and with a clear process with end results in mind. Kitano reminds us that "the curriculum, like education, is not static, and our eagerness to have closure, to touch actual products, should not make us forget that because knowledge is historical we will need to revise the curriculum continually" (1997a, p. 13-14).

Kitano also observes that, "whatever the focus and context of these conceptions of multicultural change, consensus exists that change is a dynamic process describable in terms of levels rather than as a static outcome" (1997b, p. 21). The change process, as conceived by Kitano (1997b), articulates three stages or levels of change with regard to curriculum transformation: *exclusive*, *inclusive*, and *transformed*. Kitano's conception of the exclusive curriculum is one that provides only traditional/monocultural experiences and perspectives. The inclusive curriculum adds some alternative perspectives from underrepresented groups and questions their historical, political, and societal exclusion. The transformed curriculum reconstructs the curriculum based on a significant change in paradigm or standard. The resulting curriculum challenges traditional beliefs and assumptions, creates a climate where students are challenged to think in different ways, and gives equal weight to multiple perspectives and diverse ways of knowing (Kitano, 1997b).

Several theorists (Kitano, 1997b; Green, 1989; Schuster & Van Dyne, 1985b; Schoem et al., 1995) have envisioned in concrete ways what a transformed curriculum would entail. Kitano (1997b) and Banks (1991) generally agree that a transformed curriculum requires the integration of different perspectives, the critical examination of materials, and more student involvement in the learning process (see Table 2). A few significant differences exist between Kitano's and Banks's visions: Banks stresses the need to "provide students with the social action and decision-making skills necessary for participation as agents of social change" (p. 21-23), whereas Kitano does not make this part of her central focus. Further, Kitano's conception of a transformed curriculum is based on the idea that the teacher is the central agent of change with regard to the curriculum, whereas Banks concentrates on empowering students to be active agents in the classroom.

Other theorists, including Green (1989) and Schuster and Van Dyne (1985b), also describe visions of a transformed curriculum. Like Kitano (1997b) and Banks (1991), Green and Schuster and Van Dyne believe that a fully transformed curriculum incorporates new knowledge through the representation of multiple perspectives that are discussed and viewed with

Table 2 The Transformed Curriculum

Transformed Curriculum — Kitano	Transformed Curriculum — Banks
• instructors select content, materials, and resources that reflect the cultural characteristics and experiences of students	• empowers students
• social realities and conflict in U.S. and world societies are critically examined	• helps students develop the knowledge and skills needed to critically examine the current political and economic structure
• includes the study of various cultural groups and their historical experiences	• helps students develop skills to construct knowledge themselves
• presentation of multiple perspectives (1997b, p. 25).	• changes structure of curriculum to incorporate diverse perspectives
	• encourages decision making and social action (1991, p. 34).

equal significance. Further, Kitano, Green, and Schuster and Van Dyne promote the critical examination and questioning of constructed knowledge and social realities toward the development of new ways of thinking and knowing. Banks and Schuster and Van Dyne both highlight, in different ways, the important role that students play in transforming the curriculum. Banks suggests ways to empower students to become critical participants in a democratic society, and Schuster and Van Dyne encourage the incorporation of student experiences and learning processes into the core content.

Theorists such as Kitano (1997b), Banks (1991), Green (1989), Schuster and Van Dyne (1985b), and Schoem, Frankel, Zúñiga, and Lewis (1995) have outlined the process of curricular transformation, identifying the individual steps in slightly different ways, with differing degrees of differentiation, and from different perspectives. I found these texts to be extremely valuable and compiled them into a comparative table, which examines these author's models along a continuum that progresses from exclusive to transformed aspects of curriculum (see Table 3). For purposes of comparison, I grouped similar stages together and provided generalized category headings for analyzing them systematically: Exclusive, Additive, Understanding the Other, Transitional/Multiple Perspective, and Inclusive/Transformed.

Specifically, Green (1989) has a five-stage model moving from exclusivity to a transformed curriculum. Schuster and Van Dyne (1985b) present a six-stage model detailing the transformation process. This model adds one more stage than Green in representing the tenet of challenging and testing the dominant paradigm. Schoem, Frankel, Zúñiga, and Lewis (1995) and Kitano (1997b) present a differing perspective, the transformative process for higher education courses. Schoem et al. describe a four-stage model that specifically addresses Latino/a students in the classroom. Their focus pays

Table 3 Educational Institutions and Multicultural Development Models of Change

Author	Context	Exclusive	Additive	Understanding The Other	Transitional Multiple Perspective	Inclusive/ Transformed
Green (1989)	Higher Education Curriculum Tranformation	Excludes works and perspectives of nonwestern cultures and women	Adds superstar minorities/women but no structural change	Includes content to analyze and understand excluded groups	Provides many perspectives of "reality," switching from dominant to outsider	Incorporates new scholarship, methodologies, ways of thinking, ways of teaching/ learning
Schuster & Van Dyne (1985)	Higher Education Curriculum Tranformation	Invisible women Excludes works and perspectives of woman	Searching for missing women Adds content and concepts of few women. Generally from the dominant perspective	Woman as disadvantaged, subordinate group Protest existing paradigms of woman but within a dominant perspective	Women studied on own terms Begins to analyze and incorporate women's experiences from their perspective. Women as a challenge to the disciplines Testing of dominant paradigms and the inclusive of woman	Inclusive vision of the human experience based on difference and diversity, not sameness and generalization
Schoem, et al. (1993)	Higher Education Courses	Restricts discussion of diversity to one part of the course	Includes additional information throughout to compare to dominant norm		Integrates additional information and critical analysis of norms and implications of inclusion/exclusion	Diversity of content, process, faculty, and students leads to deeper levels of understanding
Kitano (1997b)	Higher Education Course	Gives mainstream exeriences & perspectives; adds authors who support stereotypes	Adds alternative perspectives through materials, readings, speakers; analyzes historical exclusion of alternative perspectives			Reconceptualizes the content through a shift in paradigm or standard; presents content through nondominant perspective

Adapted from Kitano (1997b)

particular attention to the content and process of multicultural change in the classroom. Similarly, Kitano outlines a three-stage model from which faculty may examine their courses.

It is helpful to examine differing accounts in order to accumulate a more coherent and possibly more precise view of the process. Kitano provides an important generalization about the various descriptions of the curricular change process; she writes,

> while authors use different labels, they tend to agree that the lowest level represents traditional, mainstream perspectives while the highest focuses on structural transformation. In between the two extremes is a middle level that incorporates both normative and nontraditional perspectives and may encourage critical analysis of dominant norm in the light of the newer perspectives (1997b, p. 21).

In general, the descriptions of the process of curricular change, including Kitano (1997b), Green (1989), Schuster and Van Dyne (1985b), Banks (1991), and Schoem, Frankel, Zúñiga, and Lewis (1995), differ according to how many stages they envision within the process and according to what social identity groups they examined in their analyses. Green's process, emerging from the perspective of attempting to transform racist institutions, involves five phases toward including Ethnic and Women's Studies into the curriculum. Schuster and Van Dyne, working within the context of Women's Studies, identify a series of six phases toward a transformed, "balanced" curriculum (1985b, p. 16). Both of these models define curriculum broadly, as ranging from individual course change to institutional transformation. Schoem et al. concentrate on the areas of content, process, and discourse and faculty and student diversity that allow students and faculty to "rise to a new level of understanding, one that transcends particularistic knowing" (1995, p. 4). Kitano's model is primarily focused on the transformation of the individual classroom.

Examining Kitano (1997b), Green (1989), Schuster and Van Dyne (1985b), Banks (1991), and Schoem, Frankel, Zúñiga, and Lewis (1995) more deeply reveals other ways in which their descriptions of the process of curricular transformation might differ. For instance, Green and Schuster and Van Dyne provide process models that were formulated with particular targeted groups in mind (people of color and women, respectively), and they are models that define curriculum broadly, as ranging from individual course change to institutional transformation.

Comparing Schoem, Frankel, Zúñiga, and Lewis (1995) and Kitano (1997b) is useful, in that these authors examine a particular aspect (course change) of curricular transformation. Schoem et al. may be viewed as a bridge between the more narrow focus on course change targeted by Kitano and very broad definitions of curriculum. Ultimately, although Schoem et al. provide a broader notion of curriculum, Kitano recognizes a more concrete plan for curriculum transformation, which sets forth the specific components of multicultural course change. Unlike the authors previously examined, Kitano highlights "content, instructional strategies, assessment, and the dynamics of classroom interaction," or the "four elements" of teaching a course "that instructors can choose to modify, depending on their personal philosophies, readiness, expertise, and the demands of disciplinary content" (1997b, p. 23).

Individual courses have several interrelated components that need to be recognized and transformed in order to move toward a multicultural curriculum. According to Kitano (1997b), a curriculum transformation would involve moving content, instructional strategies and activities, assessment strategies, and classroom dynamics within a series of courses in a department, school, or institutional basis toward multicultural change. Kitano's focus on course change reminds us that transforming curriculum requires both broad institutional change and specific concrete changes within the scope of single courses.

As I have shown, a number of theorists have proposed models of curricular transformation within higher education. In the following section, I discuss another key element in educational transformation — pedagogy.

PEDAGOGICAL TRANSFORMATION

Transforming higher education from a monocultural to a multicultural institution requires more than just curriculum transformation. It also requires access to higher education by diverse populations and the deployment by faculty of classroom practices and strategies for diverse groups of students. There are thus multiple dimensions to the process of building multicultural higher education institutions. As Schoem, Frankel, Zúñiga, and Lewis discuss, "content," "diversity of faculty and students," and "process and discourse" are all integral aspects of multicultural teaching and learning (1995, p. 1). Of these aspects of multicultural education, process and discourse have particular relevance for this discussion as they are pedagogical elements. Schoem et al. define process and discourse as "speaking to different ways of knowing, or 'a quality of mind,' and ...

attention to communication, classroom dynamics, and bringing diverse perspectives to bear on content" (1995, p. 1).

If curriculum transformation refers to the substance of what gets taught, then pedagogical transformation refers to the ways in which teaching and learning happen in the classroom. It is what Kitano (1997b) refers to in her dimensions of multicultural course change as instruction, classroom dynamics, and assessment, or the ways in which the content is employed in the classroom. Further, Adams makes the distinction between curriculum transformation and pedagogical transformation clear when she discusses "the *what* of curriculum reform and the *how* of instructional practice" (1992, p. 14). Adams notes that many faculty feel more at ease with transforming their curriculum (the *what*), but struggle with changing their pedagogical practices and strategies (the *how*) in order to address the learning needs of diverse students. As already mentioned, the *what* of curricular change has begun to be addressed on broad institutional levels, as well as at the departmental and program level, with the addition of Women's Studies and Ethnic Studies programs. The *how* of teaching practices for diverse classrooms, however, is emerging as a research focus.

Simultaneously, while programs like Women's Studies and ES began to spring up in colleges and universities during the 1970s, the how of multicultural pedagogical practice was being established by an individual faculty member making process-oriented changes in his or her classroom to meet the needs of diverse students. There is an extensive body of literature regarding faculty's teaching experiences and practices in diverse classrooms (Rakow, 1991; Rhoades, 1991; Henry, 1993-4; Goodwin, Genishi, Asher & Woo, 1995; Weiler, 1988). Many important issues arise in the accounts of faculty who resist traditional, monocultural education and strive to create multicultural, pluralistic, egalitarian classrooms. These faculty accounts describe important challenges to creating a multicultural pedagogy, including maintaining authority without subscribing to the traditional rules and norms of the monocultural classroom, faculty teaching "what they are not" (e.g., men teaching Women's Studies), faculty teaching students who are different from themselves, and negotiating social identities in the classroom (e.g., Mayberry, 1996).

When the norms and values of the traditional, monocultural classroom are challenged, faculty often fear that the classroom will explode or become unmanageable; faculty also often worry about creating an "unsafe atmosphere" for their students, according to hooks (1994, p. 39). But hooks stresses that teachers working to transform their pedagogical practices away from the monocultural model need to realize that "many students, especially students of color, may not feel at all 'safe' in what appears to be a neutral setting" (p. 39). Hooks teaches from the standpoint of "a transformative pedagogy rooted in a respect for multiculturalism," and addresses the above concerns by "building 'community' in order to create a climate of openness and intellectual rigor," as well as "a sense that there is shared commitment and a common good that binds us" (p. 40).

With respect to the impact of social identities on teaching, Henry points to the fact that these identities definitely shape pedagogical practice. She writes that

> racism and misogyny structure my life and my teaching practice in particular ways. For instance, as a Black woman professor students contest my credentials more than those of my colleagues. I try to devise clear, unambiguous grading systems because students question all that is questionable about my modus operandi (1993-4, p. 2).

In the classroom, she believes that being up front about who you are as an instructor, what your social identities and political values consist of, and using problematic, tension-filled moments as moments for critical inspection and discussion are all ways of navigating diverse classrooms, as well as classrooms where students are from different social groups than the instructor. Likewise, Rhoades asserts that, given the fact that the classroom is a diverse community where students think, talk, and write, she, as an instructor, takes the responsibility to "create opportunities for students to talk about race, class, and gender" (1991, p. 35). Finally, hooks concurs that being conscious of the ways in which one's identity shapes one's teaching and achieving high levels of self-actualization help faculty "to create pedagogical practices that engage students, providing them with ways of knowing that enhance their capacity to live fully and deeply" (1994, p. 22).

Similarly, according to Weiler, paraphrased by Rakow,

> classrooms are not and can never be neutral sites for the production or reproduction of knowledge. Those of us who step into classrooms as professors and as students do not shed our identities at the door with our coats. We enter those rooms as humans situated as subjects and as objects of discourses that give us the identities we claim for ourselves and that are assigned by others (in Rakow, 1991, p. 10).

Weiler asserts that feminist teaching often engenders student resistance and tension but that this explosive atmosphere creates a good opportunity to examine the same explosive atmosphere that often exists in society at large between dominant and oppressed groups. Further, she finds it important to address students and instructors as "multi-layered subjects" (1988, p. 126) and suggests both students and instructors should respect and critically examine these "layers." She writes, "feminist teachers, if they are to work to create a counter-hegemonic teaching, must be conscious of their own gender, class, and race subjectivities as they confirm or challenge the lived experiences of their students" (p. 145).

Rakow (1991) agrees with Weiler (1988) in asserting that our social identities provide the fundamental structure of a classroom, and she also contends that this fact ensures that there will be inevitable and frequent collisions between identities in the diverse classroom. In her final analysis, Rakow finds that, no matter what strategies and frameworks faculty teaching in diverse classrooms can develop, these will always constitute individualized responses to institutional dilemmas. Rakow acknowledges that, in some ways, "we cannot hope to achieve equality in the classroom since it does not exist *outside* the classroom" (1991, p. 12). At the same time, Rakow asserts that, even though "the discourse of the classroom is not completely controlled by teachers ... teachers can open the possibility that other discourses besides the dominant sexist and racist discourse can be heard" (p. 12).

These faculty accounts help us to understand common experiences that arise when teaching in diverse classrooms and when teaching against the grain of traditional, monocultural education. Through their experiences, we are able to gather information about the ways in which faculty adapt their instructional strategies for diverse student needs. Further, these accounts help us to see how faculty members perceive their students and how faculty members perceive their students' perceptions of their instruction. We also gain insight into faculty self-awareness about issues of diversity and social identities.

Schoem, Frankel, Zúñiga, and Lewis (1995) point to the ways in which the pedagogical aspects of multicultural teaching have been influenced and supported by many different sources in higher education, including experiences of faculty like those analyzed above: "ethnic studies, feminist pedagogy, liberatory education, and interactive and experiential learning methods" have all contributed (1995, p. 2, citing Sleeter & Grant, 1987). This melding of different ways of rethinking teaching and learning in higher education is, in many respects, the result of faculty and students encountering the exclusivity of traditional, monocultural education. Faculty who value multicultural education for all students have developed ways of teaching according to models other than that of traditional pedagogy, and these developments constitute the roots of the current literature regarding pedagogical transformation.

Many faculty members have initiated the inclusion of voices and values heretofore missing and excluded in colleges and universities built on a monocultural model. Those teaching from a feminist pedagogical model have been just one of the groups of faculty in higher education to critically examine the bias of traditional education. These faculty members have built meaningful alternatives set in high relief against ways of teaching that deny the diversity of students in higher education classrooms (Maher & Tetreault, 1992). As Maher and Tetreault express, "feminist pedagogy was originally conceived as an alternative to these traditional pedagogical paradigms" and "has been defined as cooperative rather than competitive, attentive to student experiences, and concerned with the personal and relational aims and sources of knowledge" (1992, p. 58). Further, feminist pedagogical practices are associated with "progressive, student-centered, and liberatory models of education" (p. 58). Feminist pedagogy has been one of many responses by educators hoping to address students with diverse backgrounds and different learning needs. As Shrewsbury explains, "feminist pedagogy is a theory about the teaching/learning process that guides our choice of classroom practices by providing criteria to evaluate specific educational strategies and techniques in terms of desired course goals or outcomes" (1997, p. 166).

Faculty teaching from an ethnic studies perspective have the following goals when constructing classroom practices: to enable students to "view events, concepts, issues, and problems from diverse cultural and ethnic perspectives," to "develop cross-cultural competency, which consists of the abilities, attitudes, and understandings students need to function effectively within the American national culture, within their own ethnic subsocieties and within and across different subsocieties and cultures," and to develop decision-making and social action skills (Banks, 1991, p. 9).

Liberatory education and critical pedagogy also have made substantial contributions to current thinking regarding pedagogical practices for the multicultural classroom. Like faculty who practice feminist pedagogy, critical pedagogy stresses the student-centered classroom, the co-construction of knowledge, and the promotion of critical thinking on the part of students. Shor explains the purpose of critical pedagogy when he writes that "classrooms can confirm student rejection of critical thinking, that is confirm the curricular disempowerment of their intelligence; or teachers can employ an egalitarian pedagogy to counter their students' disabling education" (1987, p. 14).

The recommendations for pedagogical practice offered by Shor (1987) include: student participation in the development of class direction; student involvement in the creation, not the transference, of knowledge; teachers modeling "active, skeptical" learning in the classroom (Shor & Freire, 1987, p. 8); democratic participation structures meant to empower students (Shor, 1992); and encouragement of student questioning. In general, liberatory education and critical pedagogy are based on breaking down the banking method of education identified by Freire (1970). Freire sees the teaching/ learning process, not as one in which empty vessels are being filled with pre-packaged knowledge, but as a mutually participatory process where knowledge is constructed and critically questioned. He feels that education is a permanent path to liberation where people become aware (*conscientized*) and can transform their world through *praxis* (reflection and action). Education, to Freire, is founded on a dialogical approach whereby educators and students cooperate in the process of learning and all become simultaneously the teacher and the learner.

As Schoem, Frankel, Zúñiga, and Lewis (1995) have identified, many strands of thinking have contributed to the literature regarding the transformation of faculty pedagogical practices away from traditional, monocultural higher education and toward multicultural higher education. Yet, in some ways, more concrete conceptions of how these theoretical notions of pedagogical transformation might be enacted in the classroom are needed by faculty who feel more comfortable with transforming "what" they teach rather than "how" they teach (Adams, 1992). What follows is a comparison of how several multicultural educators (Kitano, 1997b; Marchesani & Adams, 1992; Chesler, 1996) envision the "nuts and bolts" of transforming their pedagogical practices for the multicultural classroom.

Concrete strategies for faculty regarding how to transform their pedagogical practices for the multicultural classroom are only helpful insofar as there are faculty members who are willing and able to implement these models in their classrooms. Much of the available literature about both curriculum and pedagogical transformation indicate the importance of faculty's role and their responsibility to exercise their role in the classroom to make change (Adams, 1992). Smith states that "faculty involvement plays a key role in students acquiring more empathic and complex ways of thinking about difference and in reducing bias against particular individuals or groups" (1997, p. 36). Likewise, Collett and Serrano stress that

> higher education has to date been an inhospitable environment for [underrepresented] students; large numbers of them either do not graduate or do not perform up to their potential. Creation of the genuinely inclusive classroom requires the leadership of faculty who are willing to make major changes in an entrenched, traditional academic culture (1993, p. 47).

Thus, if as Adams concurs, "all roads lead back to the faculty who have control in matters of teaching, evaluation, and curriculum" (1992, p. 7), then faculty must begin to think about how to address their diverse students.

One of the ways that higher education has attempted to address faculty's role in this process has been through faculty development programs. During the mid-1960s, faculty development programs began, in part, because of the questioning of the quality of instruction by students and other professionals inside and outside the academy. Courses in the academy had become "irrelevant ... uninspired ... impersonal" (Gaff, 1975, p. 15). These kinds of curricular evaluations might have resulted from a gap between "how" and "what" faculty teach and the needs and backgrounds of their students. Faculty development programs also address the fact that often faculty in higher education have not received formal pedagogical training (Gaff, 1975; Kitano, 1997a; Rosensitto, 1990). Further complications arise because many universities do not reward faculty efforts to develop their teaching practices (Bergquist & Phillips, 1975). Yet, in addition to being a necessary component to sustaining effective and vital faculty members, faculty development may be able to play a key role in helping faculty move away from the traditional pedagogical practices into which they may have been socialized (Adams, 1992) and towards ways of teaching that meet the needs of diverse students (Musil, Garcia, Moses, & Smith, 1995; Schoem et al., 1995).

In general, faculty development programs have been successful in helping faculty to focus on their teaching and to develop and sustain generally recognized good teaching strategies, as well as in elevating the goal of good teaching within the culture of academia. Generalized notions of good teaching, as articulated in prevailing teaching manuals (AAHE, 1989; McKeachie, 1965; Joyce & Weil, 1986; Lowman, 1995), advocate knowing who one's students are, discussing community issues, and genuinely exchanging knowledge in the classroom. These recommendations for good teaching, however, do not always explicitly address diverse characteristics, such as learning styles and abilities or cultural, social, economic, and racial backgrounds. Furthermore, it appears that few faculty development programs focus on teaching and learning in the diverse classroom (Dale, 1998). (There are, however, a few such programs, for example, at UMASS Amherst and the University of Michigan at Ann Harbor.) At this time there is a critical need among faculty for concrete strategies for teaching to diverse students.

If faculty are, as Adams (1992) believes, integral to multicultural change in the areas of curriculum and pedagogical practice, then the obstacles to their fulfilling this role should be recognized. Chesler points to the basic fact that individuals' resistance to change in general is to be expected. He explains that

> many people have quite reasonable questions and disagreements about the meaning and value of multiculturalism. Many others worry that their own self-interest and comfort, their current privileges and powers, will be diminished by multicultural advances. And still others resist for reasons that are not conscious or obvious to themselves, or that they barely understand (1996, p. 2).

Further, faculty who resist multicultural education often express strong feelings about academic freedom and freedom of speech in academia (Schoem et al., 1995). Yet, as Schoem, Frankel, Zúñiga, and Lewis stress, the argument is not over shutting down expression, inquiry, or thought. Rather, the opposite is true:

> [Multiculturalism] represents freedom to learn more and also more broadly than we have previously been permitted. It requires open questioning and speaking up in classrooms and in faculty meetings…. [T]he argument for academic freedom and also the best defense of academic freedom are to be found within multicultural teaching and the multicultural university (1995, p. 6).

The concept of multicultural change is sometimes threatening to faculty because it means admitting limitations, acknowledging that "even they, the supposed experts, must retool, go back to study, review their life's work, and face difficult challenges in content and pedagogy in their classrooms. It will likely mean that they must share some fraction of power (Schoem et al., 1995, p.5).

In addition, faculty often believe that multicultural change would be an affront to an institution like higher education, which is supposed to be neutral. Yet, Schultz responds that the notion of higher education as an apolitical entity is a gross misrepresentation. She writes:

> it is essential to acknowledge the ways in which the pursuit of knowledge has been and is likely to be influenced by political processes and partisan values. Recognition of the imperfection and the political nature of academic knowledge includes recognition that an essential component of academia is the presence of multiple perspectives and ongoing debate. Multiculturalism is an extension of this debate and contributes by providing new and previously unacknowledged perspectives to the discussion (1992, p. 24).

Ashton concurs that objections to the "politicization" of education are baseless because education already is politicized, and it emerges from and continues to support "vested interests" (1996, p. 54).

One final obstacle often cited with regard to multicultural change and faculty is the amount of work that this kind of academic retooling might entail (Ashton, 1996; Adams, 1992; Obear, 1993; Schuster & Van Dyne, 1985b; Bacon, 1996; Kitano, 1997a). Ashton suggests two ways of approaching faculty members who feel overwhelmed by the task of transformation: small, manageable change "projects," and building a sense that many faculty members are "in the trenches together" (p. 53-54).

These obstacles and sources of resistance are important to remember, particularly in relation to the concept that faculty will have to play an enormous role in the transformation of higher education. But in the final analysis, Bacon encourages us to press onward. She writes,

> it means reconstructing hundreds of years of fascinating but limited history and literature and pedagogy itself. It means taking power to construct an inclusive reality — one that does not systematically excise 90% of the human race. It's time to dig in. The change you make is only as good as the risk you take (1996, p. 364).

Whereas the previous section outlined the rationale for pedagogical transformation, the following section outlines several multicultural teaching models that attempt to offer concrete strategies to faculty for teaching in the multicultural classroom. These concrete strategies may be integral in mitigating some of the uncertainty and stress related to multicultural change in higher education.

MOVING FROM MONOCULTURAL TO MULTICULTURAL TEACHING

The models I examine are primarily those of Kitano (1997b), Jackson as proposed by Marchesani and Adams (1992), and Chesler (as cited in Schultz, 1992). A number of other theorists also present alternative models for approaching multicultural education in the classroom. Collett and Serrano (1992) detail a model based on working with bilingual immigrants. Ortega, José, Zúñiga, and Gutiérrez describe a framework and an "interactive approach for promoting awareness of ethnic identity and intergroup relations among Latinos in the U.S." (1993, p. 51). Andersen and Adams (1992) offering educators a model with several different continua for the multicultural classroom. I have chosen to focus on the models articulated by Kitano,

Jackson as adapted by Marchesani and Adams, and Chesler (cited in Schultz) because they most comprehensively address all aspects of teaching in the diverse classroom, whereas a number of the other models (e.g., Collett & Serrano, 1992; Ortega et al., 1993; Schoem et al. 1995; Schuster & Van Dyne, 1985b) have a narrower focus in their analysis.

Both Kitano (1997b) and Marchesani and Adams (1992) highlight the need for a transformation in areas such as teaching methods, course content, teacher knowledge of themselves as instructors, and teacher knowledge of their students. They present arguments for the relevance of multicultural education in college and university classrooms and frameworks for conceptualizing its use in higher education. I analyzed the models of Kitano and Marchesani and Adams to address the specific aspects of the process of transforming a classroom from (1) *monocultural* or *exclusive* (representing and maintaining traditional mainstream knowledge, didactic teaching, traditional assessment such as exams, etc.), to (2) *inclusive/transitional/pluralistic* (including alternative perspectives, variety of teaching methods, and multiple methods of evaluation), to (3) *transformed/multicultural* (questioning traditional views and assumptions, encouraging new ways of thinking, sharing of power, teaching that capitalizes on experiences students bring, and alternatives to traditional assessment) (Kitano; Chesler, as cited in Schultz, 1992; Marchesani & Adams).

Kitano (1997b) and Chesler (as cited in Schultz, 1992) framed their models along two coordinates representing the continuum of change along which a course can move. Both models include three levels of course change. Kitano's model moves from exclusive to inclusive to transformed (see Table 4); Chesler's model (as cited in Schultz) includes monocultural, transitional/pluralist, and multicultural/anti-oppression stages. Kitano outlines four educational components: content, instructional strategies, assessment of student knowledge, and classroom dynamics; Chesler (as cited in Schultz) describes eight educational components: membership, knowledge source, ground rules/norms, authority, pedagogy, out-of-class contact, conflict response, and evaluation (see Table 5).

Similar to Kitano's (1997b) four-part educational model is Jackson's model (1988), as modified by Marchesani and Adams (1992). Jackson's model also includes four dimensions of teaching and learning (see Figure 1):

1. Students: knowing one's students and understanding the ways that students from various social and cultural backgrounds experience the college classroom

Table 4 A Paradigm for Multicultural Course Change: Examining Course Components and Levels of Change

Component	Exclusive	Inclusive	Transformed
Content	Gives traditional mainstream experiences and perspectives; adds authors from different backgrounds who confirm traditional perspectives or support stereotypes	Adds alternative perspectives through materials, readings, speakers; analyzes historical exclusion of alternative perspectives.	Reconceptualizes the content through a shift in paradigm or standard; presents content through nondominant perspective.
Instructional Strategies and Activities	Mainly lecture and other didactic methods; question-and-answer discussions; instructor as purveyor of knowledge.	Instructor as purveyor of knowledge but uses a variety of methods to Relate new knowledge to previous experience Engage students in constructing knowledge Build critical thinking skills Encourage peer learning	Change in power structure so that students and instructor learn from each other; methods center on student experience/ knowledge such as Analyzing concepts against personal experience Issues-oriented approaches Critical pedagogy
Assessment of Student Knowledge	Primarily examinations and papers	Multiple methods and alternatives to standard exams and papers; student choice.	Alternatives that focus on student growth: action-oriented projects; self-assessment, reflection on the course.
Classroom Dynamics	Focus exclusively on content; avoidance of social issues in classroom; no attempt to monitor student participation.	Acknowledge and processing of social issues in classroom; monitoring and ensuring equity in student participation.	Challenging of biased views and sharing of diverse perspectives while respecting rules established for group process; equity in participation.

Adapted from Kitano (1997b, p. 24)

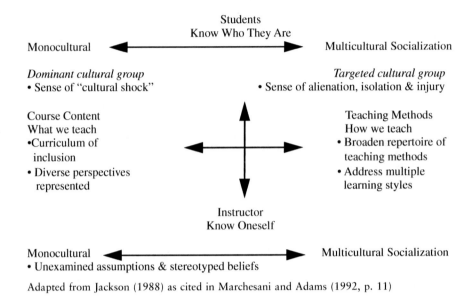

Adapted from Jackson (1988) as cited in Marchesani and Adams (1992, p. 11)

Figure 1. Dynamics of Multicultural Teaching and Learning

2. Instructor: knowing oneself as a person with a prior history of academic socialization interacting with a social and cultural background and learned beliefs
3. Course content: creating a curriculum that incorporates diverse social and cultural perspectives
4. Teaching methods: developing a broad repertoire of teaching methods to address learning styles of students from different social backgrounds more effectively (1988, p.10)

Marchesani and Adams explain further that,

> as we enlarge our repertoire of curricular and teaching strategies, we increase the likelihood of academic success for a broader range of students and we enable more socially diverse college students to feel welcomed, included, and competent. The benefits of instructional flexibility, however, (extends) to the traditional student as well, because varied teaching is effective teaching in any event. It increases the likelihood of matching learning differences for all students, while providing regular practice and development in their less preferred modes. Finally, a college teacher's repertoire of teaching strategies exemplifies for all students the multicultural value of reciprocity rather than the monocultural expectation of acculturation (1992, p. 15).

These two models — Kitano's (1997b) and Jackson's (1988) model, as modified by Marchesani and Adams (1992) — have several important similarities that also inform this study. First, they propose that instructors have a responsibility in transforming curricula, course content, and instructional strategies to support students with multiple learning styles and diverse social group memberships. Second, they establish that faculty play an integral role in changing the inequitable practices in the classroom and throughout the institution of higher education. Third, they agree, either implicitly or explicitly, that the instructor's self-knowledge strongly affects their teaching with diverse students: faculty need to examine "attitudes, beliefs, values, and behaviors in terms of their own socialization" (Kitano, 1997a, p. 15). Fourth, they acknowledge that faculty need to engage students in a variety of ways to help them learn. Both outline this process using a continuum, along which both students and faculty move and progress from monoculturalism to multiculturalism.

These models also have some important points of departure that should be noted, particularly in light of Chesler's (as cited in Schulz, 1992) model (see Table 5). First, whereas Kitano (1997b) has stated that it is vital for teachers to examine their own socialization, it is not a focal point of the model she presents for faculty, nor is it a focal point for Chesler. Kitano, unlike Jackson (1988), assumes that faculty will pursue this aspect of self-analysis on their own terms. Second, Kitano's model, like Chesler's, addresses more specific, practice-oriented issues, and it provides more concrete examples. Jackson, on the other hand, offers a model that is more theoretical and more generalized in approach. Third, both Kitano and Chesler include issues of assessment and evaluation within the purview of pedagogical practice, whereas Marchesani and Adams (1992) do not. Fourth, Jackson (as cited in Marchesani and Adams) suggests that change occurs in a process-oriented manner, yet does not explicitly break down and describe the individual stages of that process, as do Kitano and Chesler. Finally, Chesler, unlike both Kitano and Jackson, admits that, out of this change process, conflict will naturally arise, and he articulates specific means by which teachers might address and mediate this change-inspired conflict. Chesler also discusses being a pro-active instructor by focusing on relationships with students both inside and outside of the classroom.

As shown, there are a number of models charting the process of transformation from a monocultural to a multicultural classroom in higher education. Though these models both converge and diverge, taken separately and together they represent a change process that, not only envisions a potential for transformation, but also charts, in some institutions, a transformational reality.

Table 5 Movement from a Monocultural to Multicultural Classroom Environment

	Monocultural Classroom	Transitional or Pluralistic Classroom	Multicultural or Anti-oppression Classroom
Membership	Exclusive to certain groups	Others are allowed in; Urged to "fit"	Many kinds of people activity sought
Knowledge Source	Instructor Tradition or Cannon	Instructor open to students' reaction Include some Black, Latino, etc., & women sources as examples	Students and instructor interact & co-generate new knowledge Framed by concern for multiculturalism Open focus on oppression in content & process
Ground Rules/Norms	Set by instructor on basis of dominant culture	Instructor sets & checks with class "Safe" for some	Jointly generated by students & instructor Safe for all
Power & Safety	One style - verbal/ rational	Recognizes alternative styles	Use multiple styles Analyze White/male bias of "normal" rules
Authority	Instructor locus	Instructor locus, but friendly & open to suggestions Dominant student groups informally participate	Shared between instructor & students Shared among students of all groups Not White & male styles
Pedagogy	Lecture, tests, standard papers Instructor focus Instructor "fills" students Verbal/rational	Guided group discussion Instructor leadership Standard activities, open to alternatives	Co-leadership Open & evolving discussion Groupwork with attention to race/gender issues Interactions & activities to promote different learning styles Experiential focus
Out-of-class Contact	Limited, formal Student initiative Focus on correcting errors	Accessible Informal	Pro-active by instructor On students' turf Focus on relationships & learning
Conflict Response	Repress, avoid	Recognize but deflect Prevent by being nice, courteous & tolerant	Treated as opportunity for learning Created or sought
Evaluation	Stress "right/wrong" Rational/logical/verbal emphasis Uni-model & standard	Stress "right/wrong" with some expression Multi-model & varied	Focus on expression & application Multi-model differentiated for various groups

Adapted from Chesler as cited in Schulz (1992, p. 13)

CONCLUSIONS

In this chapter, I have discussed several bodies of literature that are relevant to an examination of the choices faculty make, both curricular and pedagogical, when teaching in diverse classrooms. These bodies of literature include the history of higher education, from exclusion to the development of multicultural organizations, curricular and pedagogical transformation, and developmental models for teaching in diverse classrooms. As most recent statistics reveal, students in U.S. higher education classrooms are rapidly becoming more diverse along lines of socioeconomic class, race, gender, ethnicity, sexual orientation, age, and ability. Yet higher education has not substantially improved in addressing and fully engaging the educational needs of diverse students. As Marchesani and Adams write, "we have not yet learned how to maximize educational opportunities and minimize or remove educational barriers for large numbers of our current and future college students in our classrooms and institutional life" (1992, p. 10).

The conservative political climate and other counter forces have allowed the transformation of higher education to stagnate at a level where it simply complies with external statutes or funding requirements rather than progressing toward pluralistic, equitable, truly democratic education. Yet, simultaneously, many currently acknowledge that our campuses are diversifying and that higher education must face the future by meeting the challenges and the opportunities this affords. As an organization, higher education will need to look to its multiple levels, including its allocation of resources, its stated mission, the culture it produces and reproduces, the structure it constructs, and the power it both grants and utilizes. Change can occur from external forces such as popular mandates, governmental regulations, and funding, as well as from internal forces, such as ongoing faculty development, teaching awards, and tenure that support and encourage transformational change in the classroom. In addition this also includes trustees' and administrators' willingness to propose and implement organizational change.

The history of higher education demonstrates that this kind of incremental change eventually has significant effects. Once an institution that embraced its exclusionary structure and mission to uphold inequitable social relationships, higher education has become increasingly inclusive because of the pressure of underrepresented groups and their contribution of alternatives to traditional, monocultural course content and teaching practices. In every century since this country's inception, popular movements have struggled for equitable education, including securing access for women, people of color, gays and lesbians, people with disabilities, and others. The struggle continues today to achieve truly inclusive curriculum and pedagogy in higher education to meet the diverse needs of diverse students.

Many educators and theorists have offered their conceptions of how curriculum and pedagogy might be transformed to address diverse student populations. All agree these transformations occur in stages that progress from exclusionary or monocultural to transformed or multicultural. In general, the trajectory of curricular change began as excluded groups identified what material, which aspects of historical context, and whose voices were missing, and then they reconstructed the curriculum to represent what had been unacknowledged.

My vision of curricular transformation is most similar to Kitano's (1997b), who believes that curricular transformation involves moving content, instructional strategies and activities, assessment strategies, and classroom dynamics within a series of courses in a department, school, or institution towards multiculturalism. Further, I find Kitano's model compelling because she focuses on change at the level of a single course, which might be more easily applied by faculty looking to build inclusive courses.

Regarding pedagogical change, much experiential literature from faculty exists, in addition to literature that describes changes in practice that faculty can implement. The experiential literature demonstrates that the process of creating an inclusive classroom is not easy. Yet the practices recommended are not obscure. These writers advocate for faculty knowing themselves and their students; incorporating social, cultural, and political realities into the content in the classroom; using explosive or conflict-laden situations as learning opportunities; developing dialogic skills; and creating a real sense of interdependent community in the classroom. Many authors also call for faculty to investigate diverse learning styles, relational styles, and ways of presenting material and assessing learning to acknowledge and meet the varying backgrounds that students bring with them into the classroom. Much work toward pedagogical change has been undertaken by individual instructors within the fields of Ethnic Studies, Feminist Studies, Queer Studies, Liberatory Education, and Experiential Learning.

Finally, the literature offers several concrete models of teaching for diverse classrooms. It is my contention that the models articulated by Kitano (1997b) and Marchesani and Adams (1992) appear to most comprehensively address all aspects of teaching in the diverse classroom. Both Kitano and Marchesani and Adams highlight the need for a transformation in areas such as teaching methods, course content, teacher knowledge of themselves as instructors, and teacher knowledge of their students. Importantly, Chesler (as cited in Schultz, 1992) adds attention to the friction that might be produced during this change process; in addition, his model is much more finely broken down than is either Kitano's or Marchesani and Adams'. With these issues in mind, I find that these three models viewed in conjunction provide an excellent framework for teaching in diverse classrooms.

Chapter 3
Research Design and Methodology

In this chapter, I discuss the research design and methodology for this study, including the research question, rationale, setting, data collection, data management procedures, trustworthiness, the researcher's role, and ethical considerations.

In addition to collecting data related to the primary research question in the survey and the interviews, I collected data on several survey and interview questions to be used only by the UMASS Amherst Center for Teaching (CFT). These questions were specifically designed to provide the CFT with information regarding the effectiveness of the TLDC Project (see Appendix B, questions A1, A3, A4, and B2). The fourth section of my interview protocol elicited information about how the TLDC Project may have influenced changes in faculty's instructional practices and in the way faculty devise their course curriculum and content (see Appendix G). These sections have not been used in the reporting and analysis.

RESEARCH QUESTIONS

This study investigated the following research question, with three subquestions: How do faculty who participated in the Teaching and Learning in the Diverse Classroom Faculty and TA Partnership Project (TLDC Project) reflect on their experiences and pedagogical practices as instructors in diverse classrooms?

Subquestions were:

1. How do faculty think about teaching methods in a diverse classroom?
2. How do faculty think about course content in a diverse classroom?
3. What further support would faculty need to sustain/continue growth as educators in diverse classrooms?

SETTING

This study was conducted at UMASS Amherst, a land-grant institution in Western Massachusetts with a stated commitment to diversity and to research. In the Fall semester of 2000, the total undergraduate and graduate student population at UMASS Amherst numbered 23,570. The average age of the undergraduate student population was 20.6 years. The average age of the graduate student population was 32.3 years. Fifty-one percent of the total student population were female; 49% were male (*UMass at a Glance*, 2000-2001). Seventeen and three-tenths percent of the undergraduate population and 16.3% of the degree-seeking graduate students were ALANA (African, Latino/a, Asian, Native American — all U.S. citizens) students. Although sexual orientation and disability, among other social identity groups, contribute to the diversity of the University, there are currently no statistics available concerning the overall numbers of students who identify as gay, lesbian, bisexual, transsexual, and/or students who have disabilities (*UMass at a Glance*, 2000-2001).

The University faculty also factored into the diversity of the campus. In the Fall semester of 2000, the total number of faculty were 1,458. Approximately 31% of the faculty were female and 69% were male (*OIR Factbook*, Fall 2000). Thirteen and nine-tenths of the faculty identified themselves as faculty of color according to the following categories: American Indian or Alaska Native, Asian or Pacific Islander, Black or African American, Hispanic or Latino/a.

The University operates with an expressed commitment to diversity, as clearly stated in Chancellor David Scott's statement of purpose to

> remove barriers: barriers to access..., barriers between different cultures; between different groups — faculty, students, staff, administrators; between administrative structures, the organization of the University and the physical structures (UMASS Office of the Chancellor 1997-2001).

The dramatic increase in the numbers of diverse students on college campuses hailed by educators and theorists like Kitano (1997b), Marchesani and Adams (1992), Adams (1992), and Valverde (1998) were indeed experienced at the University. Between the Fall semesters of 1987 and 1996, the numbers of entering first-year ALANA undergraduates steadily increased from 364 to 738. Since then, the University has struggled to achieve its expressed goals for campus diversity. As part of a national backlash, the practice of Affirmative Action was called into question during the mid- to late-1990s at the

University (Feagin, Vera, & Imani, 1996). The process of dismantling Affirmative Action resulted in the decline of entering, first-year ALANA undergraduates. Between 1996 and 1999 (the last year for which data are available), the number of ALANA students dropped from 738 to 596.

Even while the struggle over Affirmative Action transpired at the University, the campus maintained its activist orientation, with faculty and student groups working together towards the creation of a more diverse community (Ouellett & Sorcinelli, 1995). The Chancellor's Commission on Civility in Human Relations was an initial step in this direction. Established in 1980, this commission aimed to "help articulate an appropriate institutional perspective and to attempt cohesion among the variety of agendas being put forth on diversity issues" (p. 206). In the late 1990s the name of the commission was changed to the Chancellor's Council on Community, Diversity, and Social Justice. The Council's success in integrating awareness and acceptance of diversity into the campus experience was evident by the late 1990s when six-credit diversity requirements were added to the undergraduate curriculum and programs on diversity were facilitated in the residential halls (Ouellett & Sorcinelli, 1995).

Though the numbers of ALANA students have recently experienced a decline at the UMASS Amherst, the campus still offers elements of diversity when it is characterized in broader terms (gender, ability, class, sexual orientation, religion, first language, first-year students, etc.). It is important to have wide representation of diverse interests in an academic community (Smith & Schonfeld, 2000; AACU, 1999), and the decline in the number of students of color is an issue that the UMASS Amherst will have to address. Nonetheless, because of the literature that educators and theorists have produced in the last decade, attention now extends beyond race and ethnicity when describing and attending to the diverse needs of students (Kitano, 1997a).

The recognition of the multiple dimensions of diversity at the University led to more complex thinking about how faculty could better address diverse students' needs in the classroom. In the past, Teaching Assistants (TAs) and faculty members were left to independently address diverse students' needs. Ouellett and Sorcinelli explain that,

> in response to these changing learning and teaching needs, the Center for Teaching (CFT) and the Graduate Student Senate cosponsored a three-year grant to develop a new TA and faculty development program. The grant proposed a variety of programming initiatives under the title of "Teaching and Learning in the Diverse Classroom" (TLDC) (1995, p. 207).

Each year between 1994 and 1999, staff of the TLDC Project invited eight faculty-TA teams across academic disciplines to participate in a year-long seminar experience to aid in developing their understanding of diversity and teaching. Between 1999 and 2001, the seminar was conducted interdepartmentally, rather than across disciplines, yet the substance and goals of the program remained the same. The seminar involved a four-step process:

1) an intensive one-day immersion workshop at the outset of the year,
2) a monthly seminar on teaching and learning in the diverse class room,
3) individual consultation on teaching and learning, and
4) a department-based teaching and learning project designed by each team (Ouellett and Sorcinelli, 1998, p. 113).

The TLDC Project's stated purpose and goals work to further the University's commitment to:

• Increasing the ability of instructors to create inclusive classrooms
• Increasing teachers' self-awareness in order to engender empathy/ greater sensitivity to feelings, experiences, and concerns of students typically underrepresented in the academy
• Highlighting the impact that organizational development level norms and values have on diversity in the classroom
• Encouraging participants to make a long-term commitment to enhancing skills for teaching in the diverse classroom.

PARTICIPANTS

All current faculty members at the UMASS Amherst who had participated in the TLDC Project were invited to take part in this study. The TLDC Project spanned the academic years 1994 through 2001. It was a two-semester seminar in which faculty volunteered to be involved. Since the inception of the TLDC Project, there have been a total of 50 faculty who participated. The survey for this study was sent to 47 participants; three past participants were no longer available on campus and could not be reached. Of the 47 surveys sent out, 29 responses were received. From the larger pool of surveyed participants, I interviewed eleven individuals who constituted a diverse selection across academic disciplines,[1] levels of faculty rank, gender, and race (see Table 6). I piloted the interview protocol with one potential informant in order to assess and evaluate the clarity of the instrument. That protocol was not included in the overall analysis. All of the remaining (10) interviewed participants were tenured faculty.

DATA COLLECTION METHODS

This section sets forth the rationale and development of both the survey and the interview guide, as well as the connection of these methods to my research question.

Survey

Survey Rationale

I conducted the surveys as a precursor to the interviews, knowing that the shorter, quicker format of the surveys would provide me with initial insights but not allow for the kind of interactive probing that I would need to gather more in-depth information. Also, the data from the surveys aided in the construction of an interview guide.

The use of surveys in this study was advantageous for several reasons. According to Babbie, survey research is particularly useful for describing the demographic characteristics of a given group. Surveys are also useful as a method to "collect self-reports of recalled past action, or of prospective or hypothetical action" (1986, p. 233). This study investigated the past experiences of teachers involved in the TLDC Project, as well as their conceptions of what they would require for future development as teachers in diverse classrooms. Further, surveys offered this study greater flexibility because, as Babbie writes, "many questions may be asked on a given topic, giving you considerable flexibility in your analysis" (1986, p. 232). Finally, the use of surveys allowed me to employ a consistent procedure, asking the same questions, in the same order, and with the same intent with each participant I surveyed (Babbie, 1986).

This study took into consideration the possible limitations of using surveys. First, according to Gall, "questionnaires ... cannot probe deeply into respondents' opinions and feeling" (1996, p. 289). Similarly, Babbie states that "surveys may appear to be superficial in their coverage of complex topics. This is inherent in survey research" and

> the requirement for standardized questions ... often seems to result in the fitting of round pegs into square holes. Standardized questionnaire items often represent the least common denominator in assessing people's attitudes, orientations, circumstances, and experiences (1983, p. 238).

Also, there was no assurance that respondents correctly understood the survey's directions and/or questions (Gall, 1996).

Table 6 Coding of Interview Participants

Participant Pseudonyms	Faculty Rank*	Gender	Race/Ethnicity	Length of Appointment (Years)
Andre	Professor	Male	Latino/Hispanic	21
Bruce	Associate Professor	Male	White or European American	8
Coretta	Associate Professor	Female	Black	30
David	Associate Professor	Male	White or European American	5
Marisela	Associate Professor	Female	Latina/Hispanic	7
Mohammed	Associate Professor	Male	Other	25
Pamela	Associate Professor	Female	White or European American	5
Rita	Professor	Female	White or European American	26
Sharon	Associate Professor	Female	Black	14
Susan	Associate Professor	Female	White/Jewish	10

* All Associate Professors and Professors were tenured.

Development of Survey

The survey was self-administered and consisted of both closed-ended and open-ended questions. Closed-ended questions were developed to identify demographics and information about the participants. Closed-ended questions were beneficial because, as Babbie explains, "they provide a greater uniformity of responses and are more easily processed" (1986, p. 127). In addition, Gall writes that "the advantage of designing questions in closed form is that it makes quantification and analysis of results easier" requiring minimal effort by both researcher and respondent (1996, p. 296). Yet, as Doppler highlights, "since closed-ended questions carry the disadvantage of limiting answers to the choices provided," the survey also consisted of open-ended questions, allowing for greater freedom in response (2000, p. 60).

The survey format was designed based upon an extensive search in the data archives for similar surveys on the topic of teaching and diversity (Hasslen, 1993; Evans, 1995; Saulter, 1996). Further, I interviewed the Associate Director of the Center for Teaching (CFT) at the UMASS Amherst, with regard to developing relevant topics and questions for the survey. Additionally, I met with a researcher from the Educational Policy Research and Administration (EPRA) Department at the UMASS Amherst, who offered advice in the construction of the survey. The survey was designed to be confidential, meaning that it was anonymous to all except for the researcher; no participant was or will be identified in the research report.

The Associate Director for the CFT and the members of my dissertation committee examined and reviewed the survey for content. The previously mentioned researcher from EPRA reviewed the survey for technical soundness.

In the survey, I employed Likert-scale questions to measure attitudes. In this way, faculty attitudes regarding their experiences and practices following participation in the TLDC Project were measured. The advantage of the Likert scale is that it is the most specific means of measuring attitudes across a spectrum. One disadvantage is that the scale limited participants' response options to a defined continuum between agree at one end and disagree at the other. This method does not allow for a more thorough explanation (Gall, 1996). Because of this disadvantage, I decided to follow the survey with semistructured interviews.

Relationship of Survey to Research Question

The survey was constructed to answer my primary research questions. (A small number of the questions in the survey were designed to specifically meet the needs of the CFT; therefore, the data generated from these questions were not employed for the purposes of this study, but were turned over to the CFT for their purposes). I subdivided the survey into four categories, utilizing both open-ended and closed-ended questions throughout: A) Faculty's Experiences with the TLDC Project, B) Faculty's Professional Development Experiences with Teaching in Diverse Classrooms, C) Faculty's Experiences with Teaching in Diverse Classrooms, D) Faculty's Personal and Professional Characteristics.

In the first section, Faculty's Experiences with the TLDC Project, faculty participants were asked (2000, p. 60) to discuss their experiences with the TLDC Project. Participants were asked (see A1 in Appendix B) to self-reflect about their teaching in areas such as philosophy of teaching, awareness of diversity issues, and approach to class preparation and instruction. Participants were also asked to indicate the extent to which their pedagogical and curricular practices were changed by their participation in the TLDC Project. Questions included: A2) What motivated you to participate in the TLDC Project? A3) What aspects of the TLDC Project were most helpful to you during your participation in the program? and A4) Since you participated in the TLDC Project, to what extent have you had continued interactions with faculty in your TLDC cohort and/or Center for Teaching staff? This section was valuable to the study because it asked faculty to reflect on the skills they acquired in the TLDC Project as needed to transform the classroom from monocultural to multicultural.

The second section of this survey, Faculty's Professional Development Experiences with Teaching in Diverse Classrooms, reflected inquiry into faculty members' educational and training experiences addressing diversity in the classroom, including involvement in courses and/or professional development seminars both prior to and following their participation in the TLDC Project. Questions included: B1) What courses or professional development seminars addressing diversity in the classroom had you taken prior to your participation in the TLDC Project? and B2) What courses or professional development seminars addressing diversity in the classroom have you taken since your participation in the TLDC Project? This section provided insight into understanding the extent to which faculty members were involved in diversity issues before they entered and after they completed the TLDC Project.

The third section of the survey, Faculty's Experiences with Teaching in Diverse Classrooms, specifically centered on faculty members' experiences with teaching in diverse classrooms. Here, faculty were asked to address the relative value of six dimensions of effective teaching in diverse classrooms. Both Marchesani & Adams (1992) and Kitano (1997b) describe these dimensions of multicultural teaching. These dimensions include 1) awareness of issues of diversity, 2) knowledge of students' social identities, 3) understanding diverse learning styles, 4) strategies for actively engaging students in their learning, 5) fostering a sense of community in the classroom, and 6) integrating multiple perspectives into the course content. Further, faculty were asked to identify strategies other than the previously stated six dimensions that were effective in their teaching in diverse classrooms. Also, this section revealed inquiry into the next steps that faculty would take to gain knowledge and skills about teaching in diverse classrooms. Questions included: C1) In your own teaching, to what extent are each of the following dimensions effective in teaching in diverse classrooms? C2) Are there any other specific teaching strategies that you find to be effective in teaching in diverse classrooms? and C3) What do you see as your next steps for gaining knowledge and skills about teaching in diverse classrooms?

The fourth section of the survey, Faculty's Personal and Professional Characteristics, focused on the participants' demographic characteristics.

Questions included: D1) In what school/college at UMASS is your primary faculty appointment? D2) How many years have you been a faculty member at UMASS? D3) What is your current rank? D4) What is your gender? And D5) Which of the following best describes your race or ethnicity? I used this information in my data analysis as a way to consider the relationship between variables of race, gender, rank, and faculty status to the participants' experiences in teaching in diverse classrooms.

Interview

Interview Rationale
The faculty in this study provided detailed information about their teaching methodologies, course content, themselves as teachers in diverse classrooms, and further support that would sustain and continue their growth as educators in diverse classrooms. The interviews were beneficial because they examined a phenomenon that has not yet been deeply explored (Marshall & Rossman, 1999), namely strategies faculty use to teach in diverse classrooms. The interviews allowed for a better understanding of the context for participants' responses (Bogden & Biklen, 1992) in addition to supplementing the survey data with in-depth, detailed information (Patton, 1990).

There were several advantages to conducting interviews, particularly as they were employed in this study in conjunction with a survey. According to Gall, the

> major advantage of interviews is their adaptability. Skilled interviewers can follow up a respondent's answers to obtain more information and clarify vague statements. They also can build trust and rapport with respondents, thus making it possible to obtain information that the individual probably would not reveal by other data-collection methods (1996, p. 289).

In Gall's view, the disadvantages of interviews include the fact that "it is difficult to standardize the interview situation so that the interviewer does not influence the respondent to answer questions a certain way" and that "the interviewer cannot provide anonymity for the respondents.... Of course, the interviewer can analyze and report the interview data so that the identity of the participants is not revealed" (1996, p. 290). According to Gall, the benefit of using semistructured interviews is that they provide "reasonably standard data across respondents, but of greater depth than can be obtained from a structured interview" (1996, p. 310).

Development of Interviews

I utilized semistructured interviews, which involved "asking a series of structured questions and then probing more deeply using open-form questions to obtain additional information" (Gall, 1996, p. 310). The interview questions developed elicited personal anecdotes and other information that cannot be detailed in a survey.

The interview guide was, in part, based on information revealed in the survey responses. The framework for the interview questions was based upon my research question, as well as the multicultural teaching and learning model developed by Marchesani and Adams (1992). This model takes a holistic approach toward the classroom, placing equal value and attention on the areas of course content, teaching methods, teacher self-knowledge, and knowledge of students to create an environment that supports the needs of diverse learners.

I consulted with the Director and Associate Director of the CFT with regard to the content of the interview protocol. I consulted with my advisory committee regarding the interview format and reviewing the appropriateness and salience of the questions to be asked. The interviews were audiotaped and transcribed. I was the only one who knew the identity of the interviewees.

The guiding interview protocol was divided into six sections. In the first section, I introduced myself, presented the purpose of my research, outlined the procedures governing the research process, and answered participants' questions. In the second section, I gathered the participant's background information regarding the courses they were currently teaching, their definition of diversity in the context of the classroom, and their knowledge of the social identities represented in their classroom. In the third section, I inquired more extensively into instructional practices and course content that participants feel engender success for diverse students. Here I asked faculty to provide particular anecdotes about both effective and ineffective instructional practices, as well as challenges they have encountered when teaching diverse students.

The fourth section consisted of questions relevant primarily to the TLDC Project. In the fifth section, I delved into what further support faculty need to continue their growth as educators of diverse classrooms. In the final section, I prompted participants to make further comments relevant to teaching in diverse classrooms. This section also included time for participants to ask me any questions related to the research and provided a chance for me to thank them for their participation.

A multistep selection process was used to select participants for a 90-minute, semistructured interview. First, I consulted with the Assistant Director of the TLDC Project and the Director of the CFT in order to identify those past participants who they thought were most positively impacted by the TLDC Project. We purposefully identified participants who were full-time faculty and who were varied according to their time of participation in the TLDC Project, their race, gender, academic discipline, and faculty rank. However, it should be noted that the TLDC Project's past participants are not truly representative of the university community at large in the areas of race, academic discipline, faculty rank, and years of experience. It should also be noted that faculty who participated in the interview process did not necessarily participate in the survey.

Relationship of Interview to Research Questions

The interview questions provided an in-depth exploration of the participants' experiences teaching in diverse classrooms. One way in which the interviews supported the research question is that they provided a contextual background from which to examine faculty experiences. The interviews also more fully explored instructional strategies faculty used and challenges they encountered teaching in diverse classrooms. Specifically, the interviews explored the curriculum design, resources, and materials used by faculty to address the needs of their diverse students. Finally, the interviews more thoroughly investigated what further support faculty would need to sustain and continue their growth as educators in diverse classrooms.

DATA COLLECTION — SEQUENCE/ORDER

The following section outlines the ways in which I contacted the participants, informed them about the research, and obtained their consent. This section details the procedures I employed to arrange for the gathering of data from participants both in the survey and the interviews.

Data Collection Procedures – Survey

The first of two rounds of surveys mailed to past participants of the TLDC Project (1994-2000) were sent in February 2001. Initially, I contacted participants via electronic mail three days before I sent out the surveys (see Appendix A), communicating to them that the survey would be arriving soon and alerting them to look for it in the mail. In addition, I stressed the importance of this research and my appreciation of their support (Gall, 1996). Next, the surveys were distributed through the UMASS Amherst campus mail system.

Each packet sent to participants included copies of a cover letter, the survey, a consent form for voluntary participation, and a self-addressed, stamped envelope to return the survey. The attached cover letter (see Appendix B) 1) stated the purpose and rationale for the research, 2) identified myself as the researcher to the recipients, 3) requested their participation, 4) notified participants about how the data would be analyzed, and 5) assured participants in a statement of anonymity that their names would not be revealed to protect their identities. The cover letter also provided participants with my contact information in case questions arose.

In keeping with Gall's (1996) prediction, I believe the cover letter positively influenced the rate of return because it stressed the importance of the study and participants, potential contribution, outlined measures taken to ensure confidentiality, and it addressed faculty on the basis of their professional affiliations. The cover letter also reminded faculty that the study was endorsed by an organization that they recognized and respected through past participation. I believe these persuasive elements increased the likelihood that faculty would respond to this survey.

The survey collected information focusing on the ways in which faculty reflected on their experiences as instructors in diverse classrooms (see Appendix C). An informed consent form (see Appendix D) was included to notify faculty about the research process and protocols. Specifically, the consent form briefed participants about how the survey results would be reported and about how anonymity would be maintained. This form also indicated participants' right to withdraw from all or part of the study at any time and their right to review material generated in the study. I provided self-addressed, stamped envelopes for the surveys to be returned through the U.S. Postal Service. This return process was used to ensure greater anonymity.

Participants were given 10 days to respond to the mailing. Five days into that time period, a postcard (see Appendix E) was delivered to faculty via UMASS Amherst campus mail, reminding them to return the survey and thanking them for their participation. Following the 10-day deadline, I left a seven-day grace period to allow for late responses. At that time, I re-contacted the nonrespondents, sending another packet via UMASS Amherst campus mail, including a new cover letter (see Appendix F) reiterating the importance of the study and the value of the participants' contributions (Gall, 1996), another copy of the survey, consent form, and a self-addressed, stamped envelope. Again, five days into the 10-day time line for return of the surveys, I mailed the reminder postcard to faculty. If contacted faculty did not respond to the second mailing, I assumed that they did not wish to participate in the study. The total response rate for this survey was 62%.

According to Babbie (1986), response rates of 60% to 70% are deemed good. Although the possibility of response bias remains, response bias does not pose a particular problem in the current research.

In addition to surveys mailed to past participants, I also surveyed the cohort participating in the 2001 TLDC Project seminar. I administered the survey to this cohort at their final Project meeting in May 2001. This data was accreted to the data collected from surveys mailed to past participants.

In choosing the pool of participants to be interviewed, I consulted with the Director and Associate Director of the CFT. They suggested faculty who, to the best of their knowledge, felt that participation in the TLDC Project had an impact on their pedagogical practices and course content. I attempted to gather a diverse pool of participants across race, gender, faculty rank, and academic discipline because I believed that these social and cultural identities helped to shape their experiences and the information they brought to this research. I was able to accomplish this goal in terms of race, gender, and academic discipline, but not in terms of faculty rank.

Data Collection Procedures - Interviews

I developed an interview guide, which specifically outlined a protocol for the interviews (see Appendix G). With each participant, I conducted one interview, approximately 90 minutes in length. I interviewed 11 participants, but the first interview was used as a pre-test in order to test, evaluate, and finalize my protocol. The data collected from this interview was not a part of the collated data that I used for analysis.

To initiate the interview portion of this study, I contacted participants by phone and asked if they were interested in being involved in this research process. Faculty who were called for interviews had not necessarily completed the survey. If faculty agreed to being involved in the interview process, together we chose a date, time, and place for the interview to occur. Three days before the interview, I sent faculty an email interview confirmation letter (see Appendix H). This letter thanked them for participating in the interview process, reminded them of the scheduled meeting time, date, and place, and outlined some of the questions to be asked during the interview.

Before participating in the interview, I asked participants to sign an informed consent form (see Appendix I), which outlined the focus of this study, how the data would be reported, the right of participants to withdraw from the study at any time, and the means by which their anonymity would be maintained. I employed the assistance of an outside transcription service to transcribe most of the interviews. To ensure participants' anonymity, I used pseudonyms throughout the interview transcriptions and write-ups. I also deleted all identifying characteristics that were not crucial to participants' stories.

In keeping with Gall (1996) and Marshall and Rossman (1998), throughout the interviews I considered the importance and value of the relationship between the interviewer and interviewees. I was attentive to providing a comfortable and private place of their choice for the setting of the interview. I worked to build trust and rapport with participants during the interview process by being sensitive to the backgrounds and experiences of participants and by considering their nonverbal communications.

DATA MANAGEMENT AND ANALYSIS

In this section, I detail the methods by which I extracted and analyzed the data collected in the surveys and the interviews.

Surveys

For closed-ended questions, I used SPSS (a statistical analysis program) to describe the frequencies and percentages of responses against each characteristic of the sample research population, including gender, race, ethnicity, rank, length of appointment, and academic discipline. I consulted with a statistician to establish the validity of the exploratory analysis that I conducted, testing for relationships between the demographic characteristics and participants' responses to the closed-ended questions.[2]

For open-ended questions, I devised a classification system composed of a large number of 5x8 cards on which I wrote segments of the narratives derived from these questions. This system enabled the "coding and sorting of respondents' words" (Gall, 1996, p. 304) in order to arrive at important general categories of information. On each card, I wrote an identification number and a code that represented the gender, race, ethnicity, faculty rank, length of appointment, and academic discipline of the participant to which the narrative belonged. I used these codes to determine the frequencies and percentages of responses against these demographic characteristics.

Next, I began to examine the cards for regularities and/or patterns, which I then categorized into thematic groups. I used Marshall and Rossman's six-phase process in analyzing the data: "organizing the data; generating categories, themes, and patterns; coding the data; testing the emergent understandings; searching for alternative explanations; and writing" the results (1998, p. 158). I used a peer reviewer who analyzed the cards separately from me, and who emerged with categories of meaning virtually identical to mine. This system was used to help me verify my coding system and achieve a more complex understanding of my findings.

Interviews

I kept a separate file on each of the interview participants in which I used pseudonyms in place of names. The transcriber and I were responsible for transcribing the interviews. After all tapes were transcribed, I listened again to the interview tapes while following along in the transcription to ensure that the tapes were accurately transcribed and to reexamine gaps in the intelligibility of the tapes.

In analyzing the interview data, I moved through the six general procedures outlined by Marshall and Rossman (1998). To organize the data, I kept a separate file on each participant in which I filed two copies of their interview transcripts and a list of their demographic information. I maintained consent forms separately. In order to manage the data, I transferred excerpts from the transcribed manuscripts of each participant's interview onto 5" X 8" index cards. On each card, I again wrote participants' identification numbers and codes that represented their gender, race, ethnicity, faculty rank, length of appointment, and academic discipline. I used the information elicited from these cards to determine emergent themes and/or patterns, which I then classified into thematic groups. I examined the text to determine themes that were most compelling or salient in the study. The saliency of these themes was based on four criteria: 1) expansion of our understanding of teaching and learning in diverse classrooms, 2) contribution to knowledge of pedagogical skills that reflect good teaching practices, 3) frequency of similar responses mentioned by participants, and 4) confirmation of the themes that emerged from the survey analysis.

In addition, I was attentive to the ways in which these themes interacted with my primary research questions. Again, I employed a peer reviewer for the purpose of verifying my conclusions. The peer reviewer was asked to review one interview transcript, looking for themes. Before the peer reviewer examined the transcript, I introduced this person to the themes that I had previously generated from the data. This process was used to ensure that my thematic categorizations were reliable and that they were the natural outgrowth of the data. In line with Patton's (1990) belief, the peer reviewer also provided me with feedback and allowed me to gain greater insight into the data.

RESEARCHER'S ROLE AND ASSUMPTIONS

As a researcher, I assumed responsibility for surveying and interviewing participants, as well as for organizing, interpreting, describing, and analyzing the data generated. To gain access to the relevant experiences and stories of the participants, I strove to be an active listener and to ask a number of open-ended and responsive, probing questions. I endeavored to check my opinions and assumptions at the door, so to speak, leaving them out of the interview process and out of my relationships with the participants.

I do believe, however, that it was important for me to reveal my own interest in the research, if only to attempt to establish common ground with the participants. Like the participants in this study, I am also an instructor who feels the need to examine course content, teaching strategies, students, and the self in developing successful ways of teaching diverse students. I also took part in the TLDC Project at the UMASS Amherst, my cohort occurring during the 1996-97 academic year. Because I am interested in helping all students succeed, the TLDC Project was important to my teaching in that it helped further my thinking about pedagogical practices for diverse classrooms.

The theoretical underpinnings of my perspective are based in a social justice teaching model, which examines the ways in which social structures create inequitable power relationships in our society. My perspective centers on the idea that it is the responsibility of instructors to become more aware of who their students are, more aware of flexible teaching strategies and course content, and more self-aware in order to ensure equal access in diverse classrooms (Adams, 1992; Dixon, 1997; Kitano, 1997b; Marchesani & Adams, 1992; Nieto, 1999).

One major assumption I have regarding this research topic emerges from the work of educators such as Ladson-Billings (1994) and Nieto (1999): that traditional, assimilationist pedagogy has failed to serve the needs of underrepresented groups of students. Another assumption this study rests on is that many students have not had equal access to learning in the classroom. This assumption is grounded in the literature, which points to the fact that often teaching strategies, course content, and teachers' knowledge of themselves and of their students have been modeled on White European and male student-centered paradigms (Adams, 1992; Diaz, 1992; Collett & Serrano, 1993). Finally, I worked on the assumption that the demographic characteristics of participants would have an impact on their teaching. This assumption is supported by many, including Sleeter (1992) and Rakow (1991).

Based on my readings of the literature and my personal experience, I believed that I might find:

1. Associations between gender and participants' responses, perhaps as result of gender socialization.
2. Associations between race and participants' responses, perhaps as a result of social identities.

TRUSTWORTHINESS

To ensure the trustworthiness of this study, I utilized several techniques of data triangulation. I used a survey to identify initial demographic information and emerging themes and categories regarding teaching in the diverse classroom. Follow-up semistructured interviews provided a chance to explore these initial themes and categories of information in more depth and to confirm or contradict my initial conclusions.

In addition, I conferred with the CFT, as they have experience with the faculty who have participated in the TLDC Project and know their concerns and time constraints. Another aspect of this process involved consulting with a research assistant in the EPRA to ensure the utility of the survey questions. I consulted with these experts in order to test the validity and clarity of the questions and their ability to elicit the kind of information I intended to gather.

To guarantee the trustworthiness of the interview protocol, I consulted with the CFT, the consultant from EPRA, and my doctoral committee members to evaluate for precision and clarity. During the semistructured interview process, I relied more heavily on open-ended questions rather than closed-ended questions in order to elicit richer, more complex responses.

It is my belief that this mode of inquiry provided a foundation on which themes and categories could emerge more organically from the participants' experiences. In reporting the interview data, I conveyed the participants' experiences by including verbatim passages from the interviews to allow participants to speak in their own words.

I used several outside peer reviewers to ensure the trustworthiness of my analysis of the data. Peer reviewers helped to validate the statistical findings of the survey. They also helped to ensure that the semistructured interview questions were reflective of and responsive to the themes that emerged in the survey data. In addition, peer reviewers and I achieved consensus regarding the emergent themes and categories. In their totality, these measures illustrated my intention to design a responsible and reliable study.

ETHICAL CONSIDERATIONS

Teaching to diverse classrooms demands significant personal investment, skill, and openness to the questioning of societal assumptions and paradigms. Therefore, I made certain that participants entered into the study with a clear understanding that the research questions would probe both personal and professional territory. I clearly articulated the purpose of the study on the informed consent form, and I guaranteed that information provided by participants in off-the-record conversations would remain confidential.

An important contribution to my ethical considerations was the realization that my sample of survey and interview participants was relatively small, thereby increasing the possibility that participants could be identified. Therefore, I reported the data from individual surveys in aggregate form. In the interviews, the measures taken to ensure anonymity involved the labeling of each interviewee using a coding system throughout the analysis process and the use of pseudonyms in the interview write-ups. I did not analyze the data according to faculty discipline or TLDC Project cohort, since the TLDC Project's Associate Director and I felt that, were I to do so, confidentiality would be breached because of the small size of the sample.

ENDNOTES

1. Humanities & Fine Arts, Natural Sciences & Mathmatics, Social & Behavioral Sciences, Education, Engineering, Food & Natural Resources, Management, Nursing, and Public Health & Sciences (UMASS OIR, 2000-2001)
2. When using the *t* distribution as a basis for inferences about two population means, two assumptions should be satisfied. Hays elaborates:

   > The rationale for a *t* test of a difference between the means of two groups rest on two assumptions: The populations each have a normal distribution, and each population has the same variance. However, in practical situations, these assumptions sometimes are violated with rather small effect on the conclusions... The first assumption, that of a normal distribution in the populations, is apparently the less important of the two. So long as the sample size is even moderate for each group, quite severe departures from normality seem to make little practical difference in the conclusions reached (1994, p. 328).

   What, then, is moderately large? Myers and Well suggest the following:

   > "Moderately large" may be as small as 20 [total] if n1 = n2 and if the two populations have symmetric distributions, or even if they are skewed but have the same direction of skewness... For most situations the researcher will encounter, combined sample sizes of 40 should be sufficient to guarantee an honest Type 1 error rate (1995, p. 69).

   In the current study, the samples of male and female scores demonstrate similar shapes, and in any case, n1 + n2 = 29 (approaching the criterion of 40). Thus, the current data satisfy the first assumption.

   The second assumption is also easily satisfied. Hays comments:

> The assumption of homogeneity of variance is more important. [However,] for samples of equal or nearly equal size, relatively big differences in the population variances seem to have relatively small consequences for the conclusions derived from a *t* test (1994).

In the current study, the samples of male and female scores demonstrate similar shapes, and in any case, n1 + n2 = 29 (approaching the criterion of 40). Because the number of males sampled (n = 14) was nearly identical to the number of females sampled (n = 15), our data satisfy this criterion as well.

Chapter 4
General Findings of the Study —
Survey

In Chapters 4 and 5, I present the general findings of the study. The findings in Chapter 4 address the quantitative survey results, and the findings in Chapter 5 reveal the qualitative themes that emerged from analysis of the semistructured interviews. The overarching research question informing this study is: how do faculty who participated in the TLDC Project reflect on their experiences and pedagogical practices as instructors in diverse classrooms.

The first section of this chapter includes a brief overview of the 29 participants' demographic/contextual characteristics, including race, gender, primary faculty appointment, and current faculty rank. Also presented in this section are results from the survey addressing the following questions: 1) What motivated participants to participate in the TLDC Project? 2) What professional development seminars addressing diversity in the classroom had participants taken prior to their participation in the TLDC Project? 3) What dimensions of teaching in diverse classrooms did the participants believe were effective? 4) What specific instructional strategies did participants find to be effective in teaching in diverse classrooms? and 5) What did participants see as their next steps for gaining knowledge about and skills for teaching in diverse classrooms?

For each question on the survey, I explored the possible correlation of gender to participants' responses. However, practical constraints limited analysis of the other demographic variables. The effects of faculty rank were not explored because my main question concerned how tenured and untenured faculty differ in their approaches to teaching in diverse classrooms. Unfortunately, the sample of untenured faculty was too small ($N = 7$) to draw reliable conclusions. Likewise, because the sample of faculty of color was not large enough (N = 6) to make reliable comparisons between White faculty and faculty of color, the relationship of faculty race to teaching in diverse classrooms was not explored. A final question I wanted to explore concerned how faculty from various disciplines responded differently to the survey. Again, sample characteristics made comparisons difficult, since a large number of faculty were associated with the College of Social and Behavioral Sciences (N = 10) and samples from the other colleges were small. Further research might explore the relationship of these variables to pedagogical practices in greater detail.

SURVEY RESULTS

Overview of the Participants' Demographic/Contextual Characteristics

Participants for this research were selected from full-time faculty at the University of Massachusetts Amherst who participated, between 1994 and 2001, in a two-semester seminar titled, "Teaching and Learning in Diverse Classroom Faculty and TA Partnership Project" (TLDC Project). This seminar was offered through the university-based Center for Teaching and included 50 faculty participants over the Project's 7 years. Three faculty who had participated in the TLDC Project were no longer at the university and could not be reached. Forty-seven surveys were mailed to the remaining attendees, and there were 29 respondents yielding a 62% response rate. I include a composite of the faculty who responded to the survey (see Table 7). Demographic information was unavailable for two of the surveyed participants. Of the remaining participants, 52% were female and 48% were male. Seventy percent of the faculty self-identified as White European, whereas 22% self-identified as people of color (Biracial or Multiracial, Black, Asian or Pacific Islander, Latino/a or Hispanic, Native American or Alaskan Native, or Cape Verdean). Seven percent of participants identified as Other (Jewish and North African). Seventy-eight percent of the faculty were tenured, and 22% were untenured. Faculty were sampled from 7 different academic units within the university. The length of appointment ranged from 3 to 37 years *(M = 17.7)*.

Question A2: What Motivated the Participants to Participate in the TLDC Project?

To assess participants' motivation for participating in the TLDC Project, I coded participants' responses to the open-ended question: "What motivated you to participate in the TLDC Project?" (see Table 8). About half (45%) of the participants indicated that they had participated to improve their teaching. For example, a Black female Associate Professor stated, "I thought I would benefit — my teaching would improve." A White male Associate Professor saw the seminar as providing him with the "opportunity to explore differences in my students and relationships to my teaching materials and style." Similarly, a White female Associate Professor conveyed a "strong interest in pedagogy geared toward a variety of backgrounds and experiences — issues of power and justice."

Surveyed faculty also mentioned, as a motivation for participating, a personal interest in understanding the issues of diversity. One faculty member stated, "I wanted to find out whether I might be missing essential things about students with backgrounds different from my approach to learning." A White male Assistant Professor commented that he had "a desire to learn about critical issues in diversity and teaching." In addition, a White female Professor stated, "I was interested in exploring new alternatives for infusing information on diversity issues, not only in my own courses, but also in the broader context of our departmental course offerings."

Another dimension that the faculty described as a motivation for participating in the Project was the opportunity to connect with other faculty. A Latino Professor indicated that the "opportunity to discuss teaching and learning with interested faculty" was an important factor in motivating him to participate. Likewise, two faculty members mentioned motivations to "work with others across campus" and "talk to other faculty and teaching teams about teaching."

Last, participants mentioned a range of idiosyncratic responses that were coded as Other. For example, one participant mentioned a "concern about graduate program loss of faculty of color," and another stated, "I was asked to participate."

In summary, the faculty who participated in the TLDC Project for the most part were interested in learning methods to improve their teaching to diverse students. They also vocalized a concern for learning more about diverse student populations and incorporating this information into their classes. Additionally, participating in the TLDC Project also provided faculty with a means to connect with other faculty and students from across campus. For some, financial benefits and/or other motivations drew them to the TLDC Project.

Predominant motivation to participate in the TLDC Project concerned a desire to improve one's teaching. Faculty may have wanted to improve their teaching because often faculty do not received pedagogical training prior to getting hired at a university. Moreover, this motivation may have been especially strong among the participants because the TLDC Project's faculty were generally experienced professors. Unlike young professors, these

Table 7 Survey: Composite of Faculty's Demographic Information (Total Number of Respondents: 29)

GENDER	
Female	14
Male	13
Unidentified	2
RACE/ETHNICITY	
Black	3
Latino/a	3
White	19
Other	2
Unidentified	2
FACULTY RANK	
Professor	12
Associate Professor	9
Assistant Professor	5
Lecturer	1
Unidentified	2
PRIMARY FACULTY APPOINTMENT	
College of Humanities and Fine Arts	5
College of Food and Natural Resources	1
School of Management	1
School of Public & Health Sciences	6
School of Education	3
College of Social and Behavioral Sciences	10
College of Natural Sciences & Mathematics	1
Unidentified	2
NUMBER OF YEARS AT UNIVERSITY (mean = 17.7 years)	
1-9 years	9
10-19 years	5
20-29 years	8
30-37 years	5
Unidentified	2
COHORT	
Cohort 1 1994-1995	6
Cohort 2 1995-1996	3
Cohort 3 1996-1997	1
Cohort 4 1997-1998	2
Cohort 5 1998-1999	4
Cohort 6 1999-2000	4
Cohort 7 2000-2001	9

Table 8 Motivations for Participating in the TLDC Project

Reason for Participating in TLDC Project	Total Mentioning Reason	Number of Females Mentioning Reason	Number of Males Mentioning Reason	Number of Gender-Unidentified Mentioning Reason
Desire to Improve Teaching	14 (48%)	7	5	2
Personal Interest in Issues	6 (21%)	4	2	0
Opportunity to Connect with Other Faculty	6 (21%)	4	2	0
Concern About Under-represented Groups	6 (21%)	4	2	0
Financial Opportunities	2 (7%)	2	0	0
Opportunity to Connect with Students	1 (3%)	0	1	0
Other	6 (21%)	2	3	1
No Response	2 (7%)	2	0	0

faculty had been teaching long enough to reflect on their teaching and assess their need to address pedagogy in addition to course content. Participants in this study seemed to have recognized the importance of teaching, despite the fact that, in the tenure process, more emphasis is usually placed on research productivity than on good teaching. Faculty concerns over what might be missing in their teaching may also reflect their recognition that students have different learning styles and backgrounds, thus requiring a variety of pedagogical practices.

Beyond these issues, faculty indicated a desire to connect with faculty across disciplines regarding issues of teaching, suggesting that faculty are isolated and lack support networks in which to openly discuss teaching. The TLDC Project offered faculty a forum for these discussions.

Question B1: What Professional Development Seminars Addressing Diversity in the Classroom Had the Participants Taken Prior to their Participation in the TLDC Project?

An analysis of responses to this question regarding professional development seminars revealed that 45% of the participants had attended seminars addressing diversity previous to participation in the TLDC Project. For example, faculty indicated having participated in anti-racism workshops,

Table 9 Prior Participation in Professional Development Seminars

Total of Sample Who Had Participated	Number of Females Who Had Participated	Number of Males Who Had Participated	Number of Gender Unidentified Who Had Participated
14 (48%)	9	4	1

conflict and diversity training, and leadership seminars for minorities on campus. Females were more likely than males to have had prior participation in diversity-related seminars (see Table 9). Whereas 64% of female faculty reported previous experience in such seminars, only 31% of male faculty indicated the same. This may suggest that society encourages women more than men to find out about their students' lives and include students' experiences as a part of the classroom discourse. Alternatively, because women are part of a marginalized social group, they may demonstrate special interest in reaching out to other underrepresented groups.

These data suggest that the TLDC Project provided over half of the participating faculty with their first exposure to a seminar specifically addressing teaching in diverse classrooms. Diversity seminars have not been traditionally encouraged by universities as a necessary supplement to teaching, so faculty have not seen these seminars as an important part of their training.

Question C1: What Did the Participants Identify as Effective Dimensions of Teaching in Diverse Classrooms?

To assess the dimensions that faculty believed to be important to teaching in diverse classrooms, descriptive analyses were performed on responses to the question, "In your own teaching, to what extent are each of the following dimensions effective in teaching in diverse classrooms?" Results revealed that, in general, participants attached significant value to each dimension (see Table 10). Most strikingly, 86% of participants rated "awareness of issues of diversity" important "to a great extent," and none rated this dimension as "not at all" important.

I also conducted exploratory analyses testing for relationships between demographic variables and participants' responses to the above question. Toward reducing the number of analyses (and hence the potential for spurious results), I computed an aggregate measure of attitudes toward understanding and integrating diversity (called Diversity Dimensions) by averaging each participant's scores on the four diversity-related items (Awareness of issues of diversity, Knowledge of students' social identities, Understanding of diverse learning styles, and Integrating diversity/multiple

Table 10 Perception of the Importance of Diversity-Related Dimensions

Dimension	Not at all	Rated importance		
		To a little extent	To some extent	To a great extent
1. Awareness of issues of diversity	0	6.9%	6.9%	86.2%
2. Knowledge of students' social identities	0	17.2%	31.1%	51.7%
3. Understanding of diverse learning styles	0	10.3%	24.2%	65.5%
4. Strategies for actively engaging students in learning	0	3.4%	20.7%	75.9%
5. Fostering community in the classroom	0	10.3%	20.7%	69.0%
6. Integrating diversity/multiple perspectives into coursework	0	13.8%	20.7%	65.5%

perspectives into coursework). Responses to these items were highly correlated (α = .79). The remaining two items (Strategies for actively engaging students in their learning and Fostering community in the classroom) were analyzed separately.

Tests for the influence of gender revealed that women rated the Diversity Dimensions as significantly more effective in diverse classrooms (M = 3.75, S = .45) than men (M = 3.35, S = .57), t (25) = 2.05, p = .05. T-tests on individual items within this aggregate also revealed that, in particular, women rated "Knowledge of students' social identities" as significantly more important than men did, t (25) = 2.91, p <.01, and rated "Integrating diversity/ multiple perspectives into coursework" as marginally more important than men did, t (25) = 1.86, p <.08. T-tests comparing men and women on the remaining items were not significant.

In summary, participants attached significant value to each of the six dimensions of teaching in diverse classrooms. Overwhelmingly, faculty viewed awareness of diversity as important to their teaching. One reason could be that all surveyed individuals were participants in the TLDC Project, which exposed them to a framework for thinking about teaching diverse students. An additional reason may be that, as increasingly diverse students populate college classrooms, faculty recognize the inevitable impact that diversity has on learning in the classroom. Another important finding was that women rated the Diversity Dimensions as more effective in the classroom than men. Perhaps the socially constructed gender role for women disproportionately encourages them to assume caretaking and relational stances toward their students, therefore prompting them to place special importance on including multiple perspectives and students' knowledge and backgrounds in their teaching.

Question C2: What Specific Teaching Strategies Did the Participants Find Effective in Teaching in Diverse Classrooms?

Responses to question C1 provided only a very general impression of faculty's approach to diversity. However, the open-ended Question C2 — "Are there any other teaching strategies, knowledge, and/or awareness that you found to be effective in teaching in diverse classrooms?" — elicited a discussion of more specific strategies used by participants in the classroom. Based on themes emerging from participants' responses, each answer was coded into one of seven categories: 1) Pedagogy, 2) Course Content, 3) Teaching Self, 4) Not Pursuing Diversity-related Strategies, 5) Developing Strategies, 6) Other, and 7) No Response/I Don't Know (see Table 11). The first item, Pedagogy, was divided into three subsections: a) Multiple Methods, b) Student-focused Methods, and c) General Methods.

Strategies referring to the process of teaching (i.e., teaching strategies and learning activities that an instructor may use in the classroom to foster learning) were coded as Pedagogy. Within Pedagogy, strategies implying the use of multiple approaches to teaching were coded as Multiple Methods. Student-focused Methods included strategies emphasizing the value of students' voices and experiences in the construction of knowledge, the encouragement of peer learning communities, and the development of critical thinking. The category of General Methods included pedagogical strategies not classifiable as either Multiple Methods or Student-focused Methods.

Forty-five percent of faculty mentioned responses falling into the category of Pedagogy. Of those, 17% of faculty mentioned using multiple methods when teaching to diverse classrooms. An unidentified faculty member stated the following:

> my teaching is deliberately a mix of activities: I lecture, students work in groups, we discuss issues, students carry out experiments in the lab or field. My experience is that this mix gives every student a chance to show his or her strengths (and weaknesses).

Table 11 Strategies for Teaching in Diverse Classrooms

Strategy	Total of Sample Mentioning Strategy	Number of Females Mentioning Strategy	Number of Males Mentioning Strategy	Number of Gender Unidentified Mentioning Strategy
Pedagogy	13 (45%)	8	4	1
a. Multiple Methods	5 (17%)	2	2	1
b. Student-focused Methods	6 (21%)	4	2	0
c. General Methods	7 (24%)	6	1	0
Course Content	7 (24%)	4	3	0
Teaching Self	5 (17%)	2	2	1
Not Pursuing Diversity-related Strategies	3 (10%)	2	1	0
Developing Strategies	2 (7%)	0	2	0
Other	2 (7%)	1	0	1
No Response/I Don't Know	6 (21%)	2	4	0

A White female Assistant Professor indicated that she works on "giving multiple opportunities and methods for students to express views — reaction papers, small group work, large group discussion [and] exercises." A Latina Assistant Professor described "using a variety of teaching methods to meet the needs of diverse learning styles."

Twenty-one percent of the surveyed faculty affirmed the importance of Student-focused Methods. Several faculty mentioned that they work to elicit and validate students' experiences in the classroom. A Latino Professor described the value of "having students speak out their ideas in class [to] make sure you solicit the views of a diverse set of students." A White female Professor claimed her

> greatest effectiveness ... is involving students in discussing their expectations for the course. Talk with them [students] about what elements of the course (discussions, function, etc.) most contribute to their learning, attending to their diverse backgrounds and experiences, valuing their contributions.

Further, a Latino Assistant Professor described "inviting students to clarify thoughts and feelings and to ask questions of each other."

Other strategies that emerged within the subcategory of "Student-fo-cused Methods" were the development of critical thinking skills and the in-volvement of students in the learning process. A Black female Associate Professor "[i]nvited students ... to examine [the] impact of their social iden-tities on their engagement with the learning environment." A White female Associate Professor mentioned "asking students to be proactive — assigning projects that make them do something that puts their thoughts into action."

In the final subsection, 24% of faculty mentioned using strategies clas-sified as General Methods. For example, faculty aimed to accommodate di-verse student bodies by including various writing activities, using varying assessment procedures, and team teaching. Thus, a White female Professor mentioned that "having students write about a topic for 5-10 minutes before discussing in class" was a useful strategy. Another White female Professor revealed, "I use gentle humor in my class presentations." A Latina Assistant Professor stated, "The use of a wide range of classroom assessment tech-niques ... helps me identify things are working, clicking or not for individual students and the group as a whole." Finally, a White female Professor com-mented on the effectiveness of team teaching as a strategy:

> it would appear that having faculty from diverse backgrounds come to-gether to talk about diversity is extremely empowering. We believe our willingness to share these sessions demonstrated a commitment on the part of both faculty to create a climate where diversity is not only rec-ognized, but also valued, and where all students can feel comfortable in sharing their experiences, values, and so forth.

The second category, Course Content, included strategies referring to the *what* of teaching. This category includes responses referring to course materials, such as the syllabus and readings. Twenty-four percent of the fac-ulty mentioned responses falling into Course Content. In this category, fac-ulty referred to incorporating diverse perspectives in the syllabus, readings, and other materials used to help students learn. A North-African male As-sociate Professor indicated that he works on "includ[ing] issues related to di-versity in the syllabus indicating where appropriate topics that show differences among population groups." He wrote that "this makes lectures more interesting and indirectly touches on issues of diversity." A White fe-male Associate Professor mentioned "using media to address issues of diver-sity as well as having students examine racial dynamics through intriguing interaction in the media." A Jewish female Professor described "using texts which raise issues of diversity, as they affect the ways in which we read (e.g., *Shakespeare in the Bush* by Laura Boharman; Chinua Achebe's *Image of*

Africa). Last, a Latina Assistant Professor mentioned the importance of "integrating a wide range of perspectives into the content of my courses."

Responses referring to the teacher's self-reflection and personal experience in the classroom were coded as Teaching Self. Seventeen percent of the faculty mentioned strategies falling into this category. A White female Professor planned on "being more gentle on myself — realizing I do not have to always make a perfect response." A White male professor mentioned the strategy of "emphasizing with students (and myself) the importance of understanding a broad array of cultural differences (including those pertaining to Social Economic Status)." Another respondent specified, "[The coordinator] modeled for me a sense of comfort, ease, and humor in working with groups."

Within the fourth category, 10% of faculty mentioned responses coded as Not Pursuing Diversity-related Strategies. A Black female Associate Professor expressed pessimism about addressing diversity in the classroom: "The students are so stressed out that any attempt to further enrich the courses seems fruitless." Another faculty expressed, "One of the most interesting things that emerged out of the TLDC seminars that I participated in was that the conversations moved from a focus on diversity to a discussion of what constitutes 'good teaching' more generally. These conversations actually gave me the self-confidence to say [to] myself, 'Worry more about teaching, less about diversity.'"

Two male faculty (7% of respondents) listed responses falling into the fifth category, Developing Strategies. They revealed that the strategies they use in diverse classrooms are still evolving. A White Assistant Professor mentioned: "This is such a complex issue; in a sense, I am still trying to get the full perspective." Another White Professor mentioned that the strategies are starting to evolve from the work they have been doing in the TLDC Project.

Seven percent of the responses were placed in the sixth, or Other, category. These responses could not be placed in the above sections. For example, a White female Assistant Professor stated: "It covers it I think."

In the seventh category, No Response/I Don't Know, a total of 21% or six faculty members did not respond to the question or stated that they did not have an answer for this item. This may have been because faculty may have overlooked this item, may have thought about returning to it later, or may not have understood the question.

In summary, the strategies faculty reported to be most important were the utilization of various pedagogical strategies and the integration of diverse perspectives into their course content. Conceivably, faculty recognized that classrooms are diversifying, and they understand the need for using pedagogical strategies, such as multiformatted lessons and student-focused instruction, as well as integrating the experiences of diverse students into course content. In addition, the TLDC Project stresses teaching skills and the inclusion of multiple perspectives, which could have impressed upon faculty the significance of pedagogy and course content for diverse classrooms.

Self-reflection and personal experiences in the classroom were identified less frequently as integral aspects of teaching in diverse classrooms. It is possible that faculty in certain disciplines, such as the Natural Sciences and Mathematics, are reluctant to address issues of self-reflection because they see their course content as objective rather than subjective. Also, faculty may perceive that their social identities (e.g., race, class, gender) have no impact on their teaching style or on their relationships with their students. A considerable number of faculty either did not respond to this question or did not know of additional strategies for teaching in diverse classrooms. This may be because faculty overlooked the question or felt reluctant to respond to open-ended questions in general.

Question C3: What Are Participants' Next Steps for Gaining Knowledge and Skills about Teaching in Diverse Classrooms?
Following a similar procedure, responses to the question, "What do you see as your next steps for gaining information and skills about teaching in diverse classrooms?" were coded into 12 categories, based on general themes emerging from faculty responses (see Table 12).

Here, descriptive analyses revealed that 25% of the faculty stated that reading materials related to issues of diversity would be beneficial in helping them address diversity in the future. Further, 18% of the faculty mentioned planning to revise or develop their course content. One faculty member planned on "finding activities that will engage students that I have so far been unable to reach with those activities I am already using." Another faculty member was planning on "recasting basic concepts to integrate a multicultural perspective."

Fourteen percent of the faculty stated that they would like to continue interaction with the TLDC Project and the Center for Teaching. One example stated, "I remain in contact with the staff at the Center for Teaching (CFT). I know they are always available to me." A second participant commented that "plans are under way to have our TLDC cohort continue to meet in order to foster ongoing dialogue on issues related to teaching and learning in the diverse classroom."

Another important dimension that faculty described was continued dialogue with faculty and students. Eleven percent mentioned that they would

Table 12 Next Steps: Intentions to Engage in Strategies for Improving Teaching in Diverse Classrooms

Strategy	Total of Sample Mentioning Strategy	Number of Females Mentioning Strategy	Number of Males Mentioning Strategy	Number of Gender Unidentified Mentioning Strategy
Reading	7 (25%)	5	1	1
Revising or developing course content and pedagogy	5 (18%)	2	2	1
Continued interaction with TLDC/CFT	4 (14%)	4	0	0
Continued interaction with colleagues at UMASS	3 (11%)	1	2	0
Soliciting feedback from students	3 (11%)	1	1	1
Helping students better understand their SI*/diversity	3 (11%)	1	2	0
Interaction with colleagues outside of UMASS	2 (7%)	2	0	0
Attracting more students/faculty of color	2 (7%)	1	1	0
Improving my teaching more generally	2 (7%)	1	1	0
Trying to better understand my own SI*	1 (4%)	0	1	0
No response/I don't know	5 (18%)	3	2	0
Other	6 (21%)	3	3	0

*SI = social identities

like continued interaction with colleagues at the university; 11% stated that they would solicit student feedback; and 7% wanted to continue interaction with colleagues at other universities. One faculty member stated, "I plan to continue to solicit input from students in my classes as to the effectiveness of the various strategies I have used (or will begin to use as I continue to grow)." Another respondent planned to "continue reading, discussing, and consulting with the staff to further the very good start in the right direction." One participant described building a national network to discuss diversity: "I have also connected with a cohort of scholars ... from around the country who are interested in topics of social justice, teaching in diverse classrooms, and the like."

Two faculty members (7%) mentioned the value of increasing the number of students and professors of color on campus. One faculty described her next step as "working toward creating a more diverse faculty and graduate student body." Another said, "I'm not sure what I can suggest for science teaching, other than attracting and retaining more minority students."

Another two faculty (7%) expressed wanting to continue improving their teaching more generally. A Latina Professor said the following:

> at this point I am more interested in improving my teaching *per se*.... I also want to review my teaching evaluations ... before the summer starts because I would really like to spend time during my sabbatical thinking about my teaching. I would like to integrate the use of technology into the teaching of racism in the United States and other courses I teach. I would love to learn how to put together multimedia presentations so that I could bring to the classrooms more voices and perspectives.

Several faculty mentioned that they planned to continue reading about diversity-related issues. This is something that faculty can do on their own with relative ease and is something that is encouraged in the academy. Many also mentioned improving their teaching by focusing on the revision or development of course content and pedagogy. The TLDC Project places great emphasis on pedagogical practices for diverse students and the integration of multiple perspectives into the course content, so it is not surprising that these areas emerged as relevant to faculty who participated in the TLDC Project. Some faculty expressed interest in continuing an increased interaction among their colleagues, the Center for Teaching, and their students. These seem to be important next steps because they represent very direct lines of communication that can help faculty both validate their experiences and gain greater insight about what they can do in their classrooms.

It should be noted that a sizeable number of faculty either did not respond to this question or could not expand upon their strategies for improving teaching in diverse classrooms. This suggests that faculty either did not notice the question or did not wish to respond to open-ended questions. Alternatively, they may not have had the time needed to complete the survey.

The general conclusions of this section can be summarized as follows. Faculty responses revealed that they were generally motivated to participate in the TLDC Project because they were interested in improving their teaching skills, they wanted to connect with other colleagues, and they were concerned about issues regarding underrepresented groups. Overall, faculty viewed the use of various pedagogical practices and the integration of multiple voices into the course content as important. To improve their teaching in the future, faculty planned to engage in continued reading, revising and developing course content and pedagogy, and continued interaction with other colleagues, students, and the Center for Teaching. These conclusions set the stage for a more thorough examination of faculty's perspectives. Toward that goal, the next section explores the semistructured interviews.

Chapter 5
General Findings of the Study — Interviews

In this chapter, I discuss the qualitative themes identified from the semistructured interviews. This section begins with a brief overview of the 10 interviewees' demographic/contextual characteristics, including race, gender, primary faculty appointment, current faculty rank, and TLDC Project cohort. Next, the emergent themes are organized according to the three most critical research subquestions: 1) How do faculty think about teaching methods in a diverse classroom? 2) How do faculty think about course content in a diverse classroom? and 3) What further support do faculty need to sustain/continue growth as educators in diverse classrooms?

Although I sought to address these research subquestions by asking targeted questions, in the final analysis, any responses related to the research questions were coded accordingly, regardless of where in the interview they appeared. This strategy aimed to take full advantage of the richness of the interview data. Within each section, various themes emerged from the data. The entire interview was coded for each question, allowing for comparative analyses.

In the discussion section, speculations regarding the associations of gender to the survey and interview analysis will be explored. I could not include an analysis by faculty discipline or TLDC Project cohort, since this would require disclosing the departmental affiliations of participants. Because of the small size of the TLDC Project, disclosing their disciplines risks revealing faculty identities. I also did not do an analysis by faculty rank because all participants were tenured professors.

INTERVIEW RESULTS:

OVERVIEW OF THE PARTICIPANTS' DEMOGRAPHIC/ CONTEXTUAL CHARACTERISTICS

Ten full-time faculty from the University of Massachusetts Amherst, who had participated in the TLDC Project were chosen for the interview phase of this study. To ensure a varied sample, I chose faculty who differed by gender, race, faculty rank, primary appointment, length of teaching at UMASS Amherst, and TLDC Project cohort participation (see Table 13). Sixty percent of the faculty identified as female and 40% as male. Fifty percent of the interviewees self-identified as White European and 40% identified as faculty of color (20% Black and 20% Latino/a). One person identified as Other, indicating his heritage as North African. All faculty were tenured. Eighty percent were Associate Professors and 20% were Professors. Faculty from six different academic units were interviewed. Forty percent were from the College of Humanities and Fine Arts, 20% were from the College of Natural Sciences and Mathematics, and the remaining 40% were from various other academic units. The length of appointment ranged from 5 to 30 years *(M =* 14.9). Participants were drawn from Project cohorts ranging from 1994 to 2001. The participants' pseudonyms are Andre, Bruce, Coretta, David, Marisela, Mohammed, Pamela, Rita, Sharon, and Susan.

Subquestion 1: How Do Faculty Think About Teaching in a Diverse Classroom?

Definitions of Diversity

One of the first questions faculty members were asked concerned how they define the term *diversity.* This question aimed to elicit a general picture of faculty members' conceptions of diversity in a classroom setting. Faculty members explained diversity from a variety of standpoints. Several categories can be used to describe the different ways in which faculty understand diversity in the context of their classrooms, their teaching, and their students. I have established a continuum to describe these different categories emerging from faculty responses. In particular, this continuum takes into account the ways in which faculty responses can be viewed as building upon one another toward increasingly complex ideas and conclusions.

A starting point for many faculty along this continuum is the active recognition and respect for diverse social group memberships, experiences, and perspectives in the classroom. As a possible outgrowth of this starting point, some faculty incorporate a more contextualized understanding of faculty

Table 13 Interview - Composite of Faculty's Demographic
Information (Total Number of Respondents: 10)

GENDER	
Female	6
Male	4
RACE/ETHNICITY	
Black	2
Latino/a	2
White	5
Other	1
FACULTY RANK	
Professor	2
Associate Professor	8
PRIMARY FACULTY APPOINTMENT	
College of Humanities and Fine Arts	4
College of Food and Natural Resources	1
School of Public & Health Sciences	1
School of Education	1
College of Social and Behavioral Sciences	1
College of Natural Sciences & Mathematics	2
NUMBER OF YEARS AT UNIVERSITY (mean years = 14.9)	
1-9 years	5
10-19 years	1
20-29 years	3
30-37 years	1
COHORT	
Cohort 1 1994-1995	1
Cohort 2 1995-1996	2
Cohort 3 1996-1997	1
Cohort 4 1997-1998	3
Cohort 5 1998-1999	1
Cohort 6 1999-2000	1
Cohort 7 2000-2001	1

and students' positions within the overlapping and multilayered realms of diverse social group memberships, experiences, and perspectives. Another view faculty arrived at, social justice, involves an understanding of social group membership, experiences, and perspectives within the theoretical framework of oppression and liberation. These categories were not meant to be viewed as static but rather complex and dynamic (see Table 14).

Faculty responses varied along the continuum. All faculty mentioned elements of recognition and respect. Seven faculty mentioned elements of

Table 14 Definitions of Diversity

Positions along the Continuum	Defining Components			Excerpt from Interview
Recognition and Respect	Identifying and acknowledging the diversity of human experience	Noticing when social identities are missing from representation and discourse	Actively incorporating these missing identities into the classroom and content	"I define diversity as uniqueness. I guess in thinking about uniqueness and difference across gender, class, race, ethnicity, sexual orientation."
Contextualization and Perspective-taking	Identifying and acknowledging a broader, more complex understanding of the experiences, forces, and phenomena that influence students' experiences	Attending to the ways that students' multiple identities lead to their way of understanding and experiencing the world	Incorporating multiple identities and perspectives of self and others into the classroom and content	"Diversity perspectives can be impacted and shaped by a wide range of factors, from family life to race, class, ability and education."
Social Justice	Identifying and acknowledging that difference in US society is used as a basis for granting and denying power on individual, cultural, and institutional levels.	Presents an understanding that social group memberships, experiences, and perspectives exist within the theoretical framework of oppression and liberation	Challenges bias views and materials. Reconceptualizes materials and views points from the nondominant perspective.	"Diversity is a wide variety of social identities and necessarily includes the ways in which these identities influence and shape structures in society. Diversity, in this sense, is intimately related to oppression, in that these structures give and take away power on the basis of social identity."

contextualization and perspective-taking, and three mentioned elements of justice in their definitions of diversity.

Recognition and respect involves identifying and acknowledging the variety of human experience. At times, recognition and respect also mean noticing when social groups are missing from classroom discussion and classroom materials and actively seeking greater representation of these groups. Contextualization and perspective-taking entails broader and more complex understandings of the experiences, forces, and phenomena that influence an individual's experience in education. In addition, contextualization and perspective-taking mean being carefully attuned to how individuals' multiple social group memberships lead to their particular, and often shifting, ways of understanding and experiencing the world. Justice refers to the perspective that difference in our society is used as a basis for granting or denying power on individual, cultural, and institutional levels. Recognition and respect, contextualization and perspective-taking, and social justice are general themes that form the continuum of the faculty definitions of diversity. These themes are discussed more thoroughly below.

a. Recognition and Respect

Participants were asked to describe their concept of diversity in the context of teaching in diverse classrooms. All ten of the faculty described diversity in terms of the representation of social group memberships within their classrooms. As one example, Mohammed emphasized the importance of recognition when he said, "I look at diversity from the point of view of the people I'm teaching the material to rather than from the material itself."

The social group memberships most frequently discussed were race and ethnicity. Still faculty recognized that the centrality of race and ethnicity can vary depending on context. Thus, Rita indicated that the definition of diversity is situationally dependent. In the case of universities, Rita felt that diversity was defined primarily in terms of race and ethnicity. Sharon commented that, at UMASS Amherst, diversity does not connote the same spirit of enrichment that she had experienced at another university. To Sharon, use of the term *diversity* at UMASS Amherst seemed pejorative. She described her experience with the term when she stated:

> when I came here it [diversity] was a new word. People around the Center for Teaching used it and the admissions office tried to use it and get people to use it to mean racial diversity, but I'm still not convinced that it has caught on in the same spirit. It's almost a dirty word now; it means something else like political correctness on this campus. It's never been used broadly with the same kind of intent that I was familiar with (Sharon).

Beyond race and ethnicity, some faculty also recognized gender, sexual orientation, and class as part of their conceptions of diversity. A few faculty recognized age as an element of diversity and found that developmental levels differ widely between first-year and fourth-year students, as well as between undergraduates and graduate students. This may be because of students' different life experiences, past educational experiences, or acculturation experiences in the context of higher education. There was also faculty whose definitions of diversity extended beyond these primary social group memberships to include travel experience, size, language, nationality, and learning styles.

Andre defined diversity strictly in terms of student learning styles, rather than in any relation to other social group memberships. To him, diversity was about how learning might occur in different ways and through different means for different people. Andre felt that "teaching science ... means teaching to a wide spectrum of student learning styles, to student abilities." Although only a few faculty members mentioned learning styles in addition to the key social group memberships they used to define diversity, I noted that several more recognized the importance of learning styles later in the interviews when discussing their instructional practices.

Attention to learning styles in the classroom is regarded as an element of good teaching practice. Yet, attention to students with disabilities takes good teaching practice one step further. Although meeting different learning styles is good for a diverse group of students, faculty rarely talked about what techniques and pedagogical practices can be used to accommodate students with disabilities.

The importance of this differentiation is borne out in faculty responses during their interviews. Faculty often mentioned learning styles in their definitions of diversity, but they rarely mentioned ability until prompted. This may be because that ability is not widely recognized or understood as an aspect of social diversity in the academy. One exception was Susan who introduced ability into her primary, immediate definition of diversity. She recognized that students with learning disabilities might want to meet with her individually to discuss their particular learning needs. She also made a point of including information about campus resources for students with disabilities in class presentations and in her course syllabus.

Only a few faculty members identified religious affiliation as an element of diversity in the classroom. Some recognized the contributions of religion to diversity, but they were uncomfortable working with religion as part of the class discussion and content. Faculty members who have no difficulties honoring the religious observances of their students may be reluctant to discuss religious diversity in more depth in the context of the classroom. Because of the legal separation of church and state, faculty members in public institutions of higher education are guarded about discussing religion in the classroom. Also, few faculty members have been prepared to introduce religious diversity into their courses, unless religion is specifically relevant. Indeed, both Sharon and Rita are atheists and have been, at times, uncomfortable initiating discussions of religion. They also expressed concern about offending their students. Sharon deals with religion in the classroom strictly in terms of academic subject matter and stressed that she doesn't "deal with it in terms of religious diversity among the students." Still, Rita feels increasingly invested in taking students' religious backgrounds into account, and she has grown more accustomed, over time, to integrating religion into classroom discourse.

It is not surprising that all respondents included recognition and respect of diverse social group memberships in their definitions of diversity, nor is it surprising that they emphasized race and ethnicity. Certain social groups, such as race, ethnicity, and gender, have been given a high profile in the construction of social diversity in the media, in academic research, and in higher education. Social movements brought these social groups to the forefront, and thus, they have been recognized longer than others by mainstream culture (e.g., the Civil Rights Movement, the Women's Movement). Social groups that have received less public acknowledgment, such as class, sexual orientation, size, language, and ability, have not entered as thoroughly into popular discourse. Further the TLDC Project focused on race and ethnicity in discussions of diversity in the classroom, which may be partially responsible for faculty's concentration on race and ethnicity.

b. Contextualization and Perspective-Taking

While all faculty discussed diversity predominantly in terms of the representation of different social group memberships, seven incorporated into this definition, to a greater or lesser extent, a more complex and contextual concept of diversity. These participants' definitions focused on multiple viewpoints, or ways, of thinking about the world. For example, Marisela's definition of diversity included the way individuals view things, their perspective, and the way they think, interpret, process information, and respond to phenomena. She considered diversity

> to be really looking at the way other people look at things and think
> about things and interpret images mainly ... I think how I look at things
> has everything to do with how and where I grew up. So that's how I de-
> fine it for myself and in my work and what I try to pass on to students
> in their work. You know that they believe things, look at things, consid-
> er things, subjects, matter, material, images, whatever they might be
> dealing with (Marisela).

Defining diversity in this way allows for a more integrated, or holistic, view
of identity and avoids compartmentalization when understanding the impact of students' social group memberships in the classroom.

Both Sharon and Pamela stressed that diversity is highly contextual and
consists of the complex perspectives and experiences of an individual, that
it is determined not only by social group membership, but also by other forces, like place, time, and social circumstance. David agreed and found that
diversity has the most to do with where people's perspectives are emerging.
He suggested that one's perspective can be shaped by a wide range of factors,
such as family life, race, class, ability, and early school experiences. He summarized diversity as

> a variety of ways of thinking about things that comes about from differ-
> ent backgrounds, and those backgrounds I'm sure come from lots of
> things, more than I can comprehend having only one background. So
> part of it is no doubt racial, part of it is no doubt economic, part of it is
> probably what school they went to, lots of it actually is just family life.
> So there's all kinds of different diversity, there's probably some I haven't
> even thought off. And I know that makes a big difference in how people
> act (David).

Pamela asserted that individuals' perspectives are continually in flux and de-
pend on one's developmental stage, environment, and life trajectory. Sharon
emphasized that the logical conclusion of this view of diversity is that diversity can exist both among and within social groups.

It is interesting to note that this more complex conception of diversity
was held most frequently by women faculty who taught in the humanities
and social sciences. It could be surmised from many of their interviews that,
in general, their academic subject matter allowed them the intellectual liber-
ty to explore the complex ways in which social group memberships interact.

c. Social Justice

Three faculty members expressed that, above all else, issues of oppression
figured intimately in their definition of diversity. Coretta articulated this
more comprehensive idea, defining diversity as

the range of social identities that impact human experience and the way in which ... that range of social identities affect societal and organizational participation. And by oppression, I mean to describe specifically ... the way that the organization of society results in an unequal access to resources and participation in the society and in organizations and so on, on the basis of social identities (Coretta).

According to Coretta, Bruce, and Pamela, social group memberships, multiple perspectives, and learning styles definitely play a part in understanding diversity. However, these faculty also believe that there is a direct relationship between social group membership and the systems and structures that reproduce inequities. Bruce explained his approach when he stated:

I think is very important for me in my teaching to be able to name the structures of isms, because I think if you say sexism, it's a conversation ended. If you say patriarchy, it's a conversation ended... So I try to give the students the knowledge to look at the structure. If we're going to be in a less patriarchal society, here are the structures that we can look at and work on. That's not to say that patriarchy is to going to move and reshape, but here's how you attack it, here's how you can talk about it without offending people ... It's going to have an element of power and somebody's going to benefit at somebody else's expense — systems that hurt people so other people benefit (Bruce).

Pamela adds to this perspective the idea that, although social injustices exist and are based on social group memberships, people are also deeply invested in the concept of justice. She commented,

I think people in their souls want things to be just. Maybe it's just sort of an issue of learning and getting past ignorance. I believe there is that drive in people to want justice.

Only three of the ten respondents related diversity to issues of justice. Faculty's relating diversity to issues of justice could be affected by their understanding of their own social group membership and the implications that these memberships raise in the context of the diverse classroom. Further, prior training may be relevant: faculty who identified diversity in terms of justice had academic training that expanded beyond awareness-raising to include a broader understanding of the relationship between social identities and social inequities. When explorations of social group membership and inequity are integral aspects of the academic subject matter, faculty may be more likely to link these issues in their understanding of diversity.

Pedagogical Practices Used by Faculty for Effective Teaching and Learning in Diverse Classrooms

Given this broad view of faculty's conceptions of diversity, this section addresses the specific pedagogical practices that faculty found effective when teaching in diverse classrooms. These practices have been organized into the following major thematic categories: Student-focused Methods, Multiple Methods, Fostering Learning Communities, Assessment and Feedback, and Reflections on the Teaching Self. Many of these themes parallel labels generalized from the analysis of the surveys. More in-depth information emerged from the interviews, thus allowing me to create additional categories to further describe pedagogical practices that were used by faculty when teaching to diverse classrooms (see Table 15).

  a. Student-focused Methods
The first theme concerned student-focused methods. As it was for the surveys, this theme was defined as instructional practices that emphasize the value of students' voices and experiences in the construction of knowledge, the encouragement of peer-learning communities, and the development of critical thinking. All of the interviewees described using at least one of the following student-focused strategies: encouraging interactive learning, integrating student experiences into the classroom, encouraging diverse opinions, and having students set the terms of assignments.
  Interactive Learning. Eight faculty members described using strategies that encourage students to assume an active and central role in teaching themselves and others. Interestingly, four of these eight used advancements in interactive technology to enable their students to take an active role in the learning process. Thus, Andre promotes interactive learning by having students discuss questions and vote for responses by using electronic calculators or infrared devices. Responses are instantaneously recorded and displayed before the class. This technique encourages students to engage with the material through viewing others' responses and critically examining their own. Andre said that this "opens up the class to be a more interactive kind of environment."
  David used computer technology by posing problems to small groups of students who interact with a computer simulator toward finding a solution. He provides introductory information to students who then explore, test, and attempt to explain the information given. David described that his course involved a standardized syllabus; therefore, he felt limited to covering certain *absolutes* in order to prepare students to be successful in his academic

Table 15 Pedagogical Practices for Effective Teaching and Learning in Diverse Classrooms

Pedagogical Practice	Excerpts from Interviews
1) Student-focused methods	
a) Interactive learning	"The students come up with their own ideas about scientific concepts. We give them information and then they come up with explanations for the information, as opposed to our just telling them things."
b) Integrating student experiences into the classroom	"Last semester, I think I had a woman who wrestled, you know, and that became part of the class."
c) Encouraging diverse opinions	"[I try to convey that] no question is a bad question."
d) Students setting the terms of assignments	"I have always let students do quite wild projects instead of a written paper... That kind of pulls people into the class. I mean, they take that seriously in a way that they wouldn't take it seriously if they were just writing another paper."
2) Multiple methods	"I think my first approach is to try to meet the learning styles by presenting things in different ways."
3) Fostering learning communities	
a) Group work	"I'll assign them a paragraph of the text... Every group gets a paragraph and then we go around and every group has to tell us what that paragraph says. That's a way to get people involved."
b) Student disclosure	"[On] the first day of class, I usually ask people to spend some time talking about their identities in the context of the learning environment ... and then try to hold as much of a picture of that in my head as I can as we proceed through the semester."
4) Assessment and feedback	
a) Student-focused assessment	"I will usually let people know what the course outcomes are ... and I will provide one set of options for how those outcomes can be met. [But,] I always make the option available to people ... to decide for themselves on different ways to meet the outcomes."
b) Soliciting feedback	"Four times a semester [I] just check in informally, anonymously, with how students like different [pedagogical practices]. You know, what seems to work, what doesn't work, what's been effective, what hasn't been effective."
5) Reflections of the teaching self	"[I work on] being very respectful and very careful in terms of not assuming anything, and then ... I check back a lot."

discipline. Nonetheless, he encouraged students to have some autonomy in the way they came to understand these absolutes. He explained that

> the students come up with their own ideas about scientific concepts. We give them information and then they come up with explanations for the information, as opposed to our just telling them things. [Still] we are thorough, pretty much aiming for them to come up with the ideas that we want them to come up with ... the way the scientific community accepts things (David).

For David and Andre, computer technology was a helpful way of connecting with students in moderate to large classes. But their experiences may not be readily transferable to other faculty because of the cost involved in implementing technology in the classroom. Why do David and Andre have these funds whereas other faculty are struggling for resources? I speculate that they have had more success in obtaining financial resources such as grants and fellowships. Societal recognition of particular disciplines may also play a role in the allocation of resources.

Other faculty, with less financial resources, reported using different modes of technology that were more economical. Mohammed made class notes available on the internet and referred students to the web site for help. Mohammed maintained a separate email account for his course to more directly answer student questions. Rita transmitted class notes, outlines of the readings, and assignments over electronic mail (rather than presenting them in class). Rita also used an electronic mail discussion group and asked students to participate in a discussion at least three times during the semester. She reported that she is "really pleased" with the results. She found that using electronic mail in conjunction with her courses

> sort of democratizes things a little bit too because you know they get it in the middle of the night and in their rooms, so it also relates to their real lives in a way that just sitting in the classroom doesn't (Rita).

Rita found electronic mail to be particularly useful in making things easier for the students who are struggling, in the way that it helped build connections between the material and students' daily lives.

Not all faculty rely on computer technology. Two participants described using low-tech games and exercises as strategies to actively engage their students. For example, Sharon asked student groups to select the name of a racial/ethnic group and develop questions relevant to the course material. Using a Jeopardy!-style format, she had the groups pose questions to their peers. Each correct answer gained a team points. Sharon stated that, as students construct questions from the standpoint of other racial/ethnic groups, they begin to understand diverse perspectives. She also found that the competitive nature of the game also motivates students to participate actively in their learning. Like Susan, Sharon used game-show formatting and role playing to involve students. Both Sharon and Susan set up in-class debates to help students personally interact with course content and own the material by having to explain and defend it from a particular position. Importantly, both also noted that this strategy is less effective in large classes than it is in small classes because it is difficult to keep large numbers of students productively engaged in a small group activity. Susan and Sharon used a more peer-oriented form of interactive learning than David and Andre. I wonder if these differences had a relationship to the gender, discipline, and/or individual teaching style of faculty.

Three interviewees described using the Socratic method of posing carefully constructed questions to help learners discover the inconsistencies in their original assertions (Garlikov, 2000). For example, Mohammed and Sharon asked students questions that help them to grapple with the course material in critical and engaged ways. Marisela reported that she asked students guided questions to encourage them to consider alternative ways of viewing material and to explore how social identities impact the way information is presented.

Integrating Student Experiences into the Classroom. A second set of student-focused methods centers on integrating student experiences into the classroom. Five faculty members commented that they used student experiences to forge links between class material and students' perceptions of the real world. Rita recognized the importance of this strategy because she has struggled with convincing students that certain questions are significant and relevant to their lives, even though they seem dry. For example, students may not believe that bureaucratization impacts them, though she believes the phenomenon shapes their lives.

> You know the worst thing is that they're coming from completely different places I think. And so to kind of get everybody on the same page ... you know, not to make everybody alike but to get everybody, if not asking the same question, at least understanding why this question is significant. [Not understandable] make a big deal about bureaucracy and so the effort I had to put in was showing that, you know, this is not a boring topic. This is about how your entire life is bureaucratized and the place you're going to work is probably going to be a bureaucracy (Rita).

Rita also commented that she tried to connect class material to people's ethical perspectives. In one of her class discussions, she encouraged students to use their religious perspectives to think about and discuss the subject of violence. Similarly, Sharon reported that she involved students in the class by demonstrating the ways that theoretical concepts relate to their everyday opinions and beliefs. For example, she invited students to consider how public policies, such as tax breaks for married couples, might impact people differently as a function of their relationship status.

Bruce used an experiential strategy to introduce difficult course material, such as racism. First, he presented and encouraged students to think about a concept that they can personally relate to (e.g., discrimination toward young people, or ageism). He encouraged students to bring their own experiences to bear on every issue the class discussed. He then progressed to an increasingly challenging concept (e.g., sexism). Last, he moved to the issue that he finds most difficult for students to discuss, racism. He stated,

> so they're talking, talking, talking, and I say, "Okay, we've got 30 seconds left. Let's do one more. Let's do racism. Talk about the last time that you participated in an act that was racist." Absolutely quiet. Absolutely quiet (Bruce).

He uses this experience to demonstrate that people are afraid to talk about racism, or at least to articulate their participation in it, and to introduce his lecture about how to grapple with it. "It's a very powerful moment," he finds.

A related strategy concerned personalizing the material through intermediary methods. One faculty member, Susan, reported that she brought in diverse speakers to help put a human face on issues that might not be personally relevant to students. Also, Susan employed videos dealing with topics that make students uncomfortable in order to promote discussion. She states,

> I'll show a video clip ... and it kind of puts it out there. It says, "Okay, these people are racist," rather than my saying, "You're racist, and here's all the ways you are" ... They can analyze it as a situation out there ... and then, by virtue of doing that, reflect back on their own behaviors (Susan).

Faculty also discussed some challenges related to the use of student experiences in the classroom. Pamela expressed concerns about "tokenizing" students and pressuring them to be the sole representative members of their group. Pamela pointed out that it can be "extremely challenging" to recognize people's experiences as group members but, meanwhile, remain sensitive to the knowledge that they do not, by themselves, represent any one social group. She noted that balancing recognition with sensitivity can be particularly problematic when there is only one person of a certain social category in the classroom. "I still don't have a solution to this," she commented. In a related point, Bruce articulated that using student experiences to talk about race can be challenging because his classes are dominated by White students. He handled this challenge by getting students to talk about "the construction of whiteness [sic]... You get White folks talking about who they are and what they gave up to become White." Last, Sharon noted that integrating student experiences into the classroom can be challenging in large classrooms because large classrooms permit less personal interaction.

Faculty used a variety of strategies to engage students in discussion of sensitive issues. I noted that although strategies differed, all reported success in creating an environment conducive to student disclosure. I believe this is because faculty refrained from confronting students directly about sensitive issues. Instead, they used strategies to help students focus on the experiences of others, thus providing them with a mirror from which they could reflect safely on their own lives, thereby giving them the necessary distance to develop self-awareness.

It may be that an important impetus for faculty's soliciting students' experiences in the classroom is the disconnect students often sense between course material and their everyday lives. When students take ownership over the information presented in class, they may connect more thoroughly to that information and use it more productively in the future. Integrating student experiences into the classroom seems to be part of a larger strategy that faculty use to humanize material that can be alienating and abstract. The faculty discussed in this section mentioned taking a nurturing approach towards students in their classrooms, and they were adept at making students' experiences the focal point of their classroom discourse.

Encouraging Diverse and Unpopular Opinions. Another aspect of student-focused methods involves the soliciting of diverse and unpopular opinions. Both David and Mohammed emphasized that they encouraged diverse responses to their questions, even in instances when these responses were inaccurate. Mohammed endeavored to convey the message that "no question is a bad question." However, he found this strategy is less effective with large classes. In a related point, Marisela encouraged diverse and sometimes unpopular opinions by teaching students to critically engage with the work of other students in a way that is positive and productive.

Encouraging diverse and unpopular views could be important for making students feel less intimidated about brainstorming and problem solving. In large classrooms, however, it may be more difficult to create an environment where students feel comfortable expressing unpopular opinions because of peer pressure or fear of speaking in a large group. One view counsels that the auditorium seating of lecture-based classrooms may keep students isolated from learning about diverse experiences. On the other hand, the anonymity of the large classroom may encourage some students to disclose uncomfortable and challenging material more freely.

Students Setting the Terms of Assignments. A fourth set of student-focused methods involves student participation in setting the terms of assignments. Four faculty members reported that they allowed students significant freedom to choose the topics and terms of their class work. Coretta's approach is a good example. She stated,

> I will usually let people know what the course outcomes are ... and I will provide one set of options for how those outcomes can be met. [But,] I always make the option available to people in the class to decide for themselves on different ways to meet the outcomes for the class (Coretta).

In a related approach, Susan and Pamela both asked students to tailor their own projects and assignments, allowing them to choose topics and materials that interest them:

> they had to pick some aspect of human development that they were most intrigued with. Then I asked them to pick someplace, some lab, my research or any of their own research and give a real life example of how it works or doesn't work, and what do we know, what do we do not know (Pamela).

Similarly, Rita allowed students to structure their own projects. She noted, "I have always let students do quite wild projects instead of a written paper ... That kind of pulls people into class. I mean, they take that seriously in a way that they wouldn't take it seriously if they were just writing another paper." Faculty argued that giving students relative autonomy in designing the terms of their work promotes a sense of ownership and personal connection that may enhance their learning.

Faculty were also interested in permitting students to set their own pace in achieving class goals, even though the nature of those goals might be relatively fixed. Both David and Andre used a computerized homework system that allows students to progress at their own speed, attempting problems as many times as they like, and both provided tutoring as a supplement to this homework system. Andre believed computerized homework helps struggling students by reducing their failure rates, since students can attempt problems again and again until they solve them — without penalty and in a comfortable environment of their choosing. This strategy may prove successful for David and Andre because allowing students to learn from their mistakes and avoid the penalty of "getting the wrong answer" in the classroom might help alleviate stress and encourage a more productive learning setting.

Nevertheless, Coretta and Rita also expressed that providing students with greater autonomy in setting the terms of their work is not without its challenges. Coretta struggled with communicating to students that, although she permits flexibility in their approach to meeting course outcomes, the outcomes themselves (e.g., understanding a theory) are fixed. As an example of her struggles, Coretta stated,

> there are some things that don't work. For instance, I had a student who really, you know, whose perspective was that theory is for other people not for him. [He said] 'I'm just not interested in theory. I don't want to know about theory.' And my perspective was, that would work if you weren't in a graduate program, but in a graduate program one of the anticipated outcomes is that you become familiar with theory and in this case these theories. So that's a necessary condition (Coretta).

Also, Coretta related that students often question the fairness of different students meeting course outcomes in different ways. Rita believed that it is an important part of granting students autonomy to not set completion dates for course work, but she also identified problems associated with this approach. In her course, there is no penalty for turning work in late. However, if students fail to turn in their work, they do not pass the course. She has found that often students do not have the discipline required to monitor their own progress.

Rita and two other faculty mentioned the issue of student professionalism in relation to students setting the terms of their work. Rita, Marisela, and Andre indicated that, although they want and expect students to function as professionals, students do not always comply. Students may want extended deadlines, lighter workloads, or other special favors that faculty feel are inappropriate. Marisela and Rita both believed that, without the kind of self-discipline necessary to set the terms of their own work, students might encounter difficulties in the workplace after graduation.

One goal of academia is to encourage independent thinking and exploration. However, faculty struggled with their inclination to allow students high degrees of freedom in the face of frequent student resistance. This resistance may be a result of the socialization of students in primary and secondary school systems and the relative lack of autonomy they experience in these settings. It seems important to establish a balance between structure and autonomy to address students effectively at their current developmental levels.

b. Multiple Methods

Multiple methods, or the use of varying teaching methods and mediums in class meetings, emerged as the second key theme in the interviews. Most interviewees (six) reported using a range of instructional formats to match the range of student learning styles. Faculty described experimenting with storytelling, small group work, large group work, formal and informal in-class writing, multiple media, computers, and guest lectures. Several interviewees explicitly recognized the utility of multiple methods in teaching to diverse populations. For example, Mohammed commented, "I think my first approach is to try to meet the learning styles by presenting things in different ways." Faculty also described using multiple methods to keep the class "awake" or interested.

In a variant of this idea, two faculty described coping with diversity by providing multiple explanations of the same material. David stated, "Some people connect well to a particular instructor, and some people don't. So ... I'll generally try to explain particularly important things two or three different ways before going on, to try to get around that." Similarly, Mohammed described presenting the same information as contained in the book, but in a completely different order, "so the students get two different perspectives on the same information." In a related point, Susan stated that, as a supplement to her lectures, she has course teaching assistants (TAs) produce their own class notes and outlines, which are then made available at the library.

A majority of the faculty mentioned that the use of multiple methods is an important way to engage diverse students in the learning process. Faculty probably mentioned multiple methods because this technique was specifically addressed in the TLDC Project readings and seminars. Multiple methods might also be appealing to faculty because it offers a tangible strategy for conveying theoretical concepts to students with different learning styles. More generally, faculty remarked that students respond well to variety, a well-known principle of good teaching. Seeing success at work may have encouraged faculty to make repeated use of this strategy.

c. Fostering a Learning Community

Building community was the third key thematic category that emerged from faculty interviews. Responses in the survey data confirmed that faculty value building community as an important dimension of accommodating diversity in the classroom. Fostering community in this context refers to establishing relationships and creating networks among students and between students and faculty in and outside of the classroom. A majority of the faculty displayed strong motivations to building community. Faculty discussed various strategies for creating community, including, most centrally, group work and student disclosure.

Group Work. Four faculty described using small-group work as a way to help students learn about and create relationships with their peers. Rita described how she often breaks the class into groups of two or three and assigns each group a portion of the text to summarize. Rita pointed out that group work 1) "opens up the class" because students "feel more comfortable talking to each other [than they do talking to the teacher] and sort of objecting and disagreeing," 2) challenges the class (through competition) to produce better work, 3) forges bonds among students, and 4) encourages students to "learn to work with somebody else to accomplish something."

Like Rita, Susan described using group work to build community. Susan commented that group work "foster(s) community because people are providing support." She employed scavenger hunts, conflict simulations, and teamwork exercises, all of which require students to "rely on each other to solve a particular problem." This strategy seems useful because it addresses the pitfalls of working in isolation and allows students to learn constructively from each other. In all of her course activities, Susan encouraged students to engage in cooperative interaction and reflective writing, which fosters relationships among the students and facilitates their ability to establish relationships outside the classroom.

Andre described using group work in his assessment of students. On his final exam, Andre first asks students to work on questions individually. He then collects their answers and randomly breaks students into small groups. Students then work on the exam collectively. Scores from both individual and group work go toward the students' final exam grades. Andre has found this strategy useful because the course material is difficult (answers are either right or wrong); therefore, students who are struggling benefit from working with their more advanced classmates. Students who have already mastered the material may also benefit from guiding others toward solutions. One disadvantage to this strategy may be that students who excel in the course may be reluctant to help other students because they fail to see the benefit of doing so. Still, Andre viewed small-group work as a learning experience for students, one that students indicate they enjoy.

Though many faculty members favored group work, they also recognized its challenges. Four commented on the composition of students' social identities within work groups. Andre and David reported that, when there are more men than women in a small group, women feel intimidated. Andre summarized this point when he stated,

> I have females who come up to me and say, "Well I couldn't get any-where with these guys. They just won't listen to me." So whenever I can, even though it's randomized, I try to ... put at least two women together in the group, and it works much better that way.

Andre, David, and Coretta all took students' social identities into account when composing small work groups. They managed group composition in order to expose students to alternative ways of thinking, to create balanced representation, and to bring together the collective knowledge of different social groups. Coretta also supported students in attempting to "identify strategies that [allow them to] own, acknowledge, and ... successfully work across differences." She suggested that awareness is a necessary first step in this process. However, she stressed that awareness alone is not sufficient. Skills are also important: "It requires a lot of practice and coaching and support for people to actually effectively work across differences."

Coretta pointed out that, when work groups are comprised of diverse students, accommodating to their social identities can be especially difficult. This difficulty can be heightened when teaching about issues of diversity, since the "complexities are multiplied." She states, "You've got ... content and process and group, and there's a layering, you know. It's a three-dimensional matrix. No, not three, it's a multidimensional matrix." Coretta feels that, some days, she cannot manage all of the dimensions at once.

In contrast, Marisela advocated against managing the composition of work groups. In support of her opinion, she described an ineffective peer review session she conducted, commenting that students felt "too restricted" in the mixed composition groups she had arranged. When she tried the assignment again, allowing students to form their own groups, she found it to be more effective.

I wonder why Marisela was the only participant who reported difficulties with managing social identities in work groups. Marisela's unique difficulty with this strategy could be attributed to her particular student group or her particular field. Or, is it that students are wary of sharing sensitive information with people who are different from them but find comfort in like-minded classmates?

Student Disclosure. Five faculty members related that they promote student self-disclosure to foster community and to guide student learning. Mohammed and Pamela described leading students to talk about their identities and experiences by creating a conducive class setting. Mohammed commented that he tries to hold as much of a picture of each student in his mind as possible throughout the semester. In one class, Pamela arranged the tables in a circle and provided food. She found that students began talking to each other rather than just to her. Pamela used disclosure to build more group cohesion in the classroom, whereas Mohammed used this strategy primarily to learn more about his students.

When teaching large lecture classes, Susan and Sharon utilized student self-disclosure in a more structured manner. Susan presented overhead projections with the pictures of three or four students and descriptions of their interests. Sharon asked students to introduce themselves to each other early in the semester and instructed them, even at the end of the semester, "If you don't know the name of everybody in your group, make sure you introduce yourselves."

Bruce recognized that it may be difficult for students to disclose information about themselves in the context of a large lecture class. In response to this challenge, Bruce attempted to make it easier for students to talk to him outside of the classroom. Specifically, he cordially invited students into his office and established rapport by asking about their lives (e.g., where they were from, what their mother does). He attempted to draw them into confidence and created a more comfortable atmosphere by offering them a cookie from his cookie jar. He stated, "I will have them come in and sit down ... and then, before they know it, they've got their friend in the room and we're sitting there having a conversation, and it's like the living room." He felt that this strategy works well in helping students reach out to him.

Bruce also expressed that he looks for moments in students' work and performance that he can highlight (e.g., reading aloud from their paper to the class), which is particularly useful when he has not yet interacted on a personal level with a student in a large class. Last, Bruce mentioned that his department as a whole has a policy to not shut office doors during the school day, and this availability helps forge relationships between faculty and students. In general, Bruce's strategies recognized and helped to reduce the reluctance of students to disclose information about themselves that aids in the learning process.

It is surprising that more faculty members did not discuss this particular strategy of promoting student self-disclosure, given the fact that their past responses indicated attentiveness to bringing students' experiences into the classroom. Since this strategy appeared to create a learning environment is less divorced from students' everyday life with relative ease, it is again surprising that more faculty did not mention using it to foster community.

In contrast to these views, several faculty members expressed that, at times, they tried to *avoid* self-disclosure. Whereas Bruce encouraged students' self-disclosure outside of the classroom, he commented that he found it difficult to "deal with students pouring their hearts out" in the setting of a small class, so he prefers — and performs better in — large classes. Bruce's discomfort with self-disclosure seems to stem from his feeling unskilled at handling the emotional expressions of students' personal experience in the class setting. Bruce expressed a belief that academic discourse should be open to anyone and the concern that prioritizing personal experience may leave some students feeling excluded from the discussion of certain topics. Similarly, David and Andre did not encourage student self-disclosure because they did not feel that it relates to their course material.

Are students shortchanged by a lack of opportunity for self-disclosure in the classroom? I believe that, while some students may not need to self-disclose in the classroom, others do best when they are encouraged to see themselves in connection to others and to build a sense of peer community. While Bruce's strategy of connecting to students outside the classroom may be helpful in building one-on-one relationships, it probably does not create a sense of peer community in the classroom.

d. Assessment and Feedback

The fourth key theme emerging in faculty interviews concerned assessment. Faculty responses in the interviews suggest that assessment is of notable importance. Assessment and feedback are necessary parts of the learning process and involve an evaluation of progress toward a learning goal.

Student-focused Assessment. Student-focused assessment occurs when faculty use assessment measures flexibly and with careful consideration of the diverse range of social identities, abilities, and experiences of their students. For example, nearly all (nine) of the faculty described varying their assessment methods to accommodate diverse perspectives and abilities.

Pamela and Coretta both established learning outcomes for their students, but they offered students a chance to design plans for fulfilling these goals and being assessed on their performance. For example, Pamela asked students at the beginning of the class to look at the syllabus and tell her if they think any of the assessment methods will put them at a disadvantage. Similarly, Coretta presented one suggestion for fulfilling course outcomes but left students the option for creating a learning contract, outlining their own paths toward fulfilling course goals.

Pamela and Coretta insisted that primary importance be placed on students' meeting the learning goals of the course. The paths they chose toward achieving those goals were of secondary importance. Both found student-focused assessment especially appropriate for smaller classes. These faculty members further noted that, in addition to class size, a consideration associated with this strategy is that students may feel that the lack of standardization in meeting course requirements will result in inequities between students' efforts and grades. Another challenge, reported by Coretta, is that students may not always choose writing as a means of meeting their learning outcomes, which conflicts with the increasing importance of writing in her department. Last, Pamela commented that students are not always honest about "what they really can do versus what they want to do." As a consequence, she is "a bit more rigid [than she would like to be] at the undergraduate level," though she does permit "different ways" of taking a test (e.g., flexible time limits).

Andre and Sharon commented that they adjust their grading to accommodate to diversity in ability and preparation. To elaborate, Sharon specified that she addresses the gap she perceives between the performance of White students and students of color by allotting a substantial portion of students' grades to participation. Sharon noticed that the majority of students of color in her course were not performing in the top third of the class. She suggested that underfunded schools and language barriers might be impeding their progress. To address this problem, Sharon formally and informally graded students on classroom participation. Perhaps Sharon believes that a more relational, expressive option works in helping to engage students of color who may feel alienated by traditional measures of assessment, such as writing papers and multiple-choice exams. She stated that "making students come to class and making them talk ... has helped a lot of students, I think, and it's helped me keep apprised of how they're doing."

Andre also saw the rewarding of classroom participation as an accommodation for diversity, but he defines diversity primarily in terms of differing student abilities. He allots about one sixth of students' grades to class attendance and participation, allowing students four absences without penalty (and more than four in special situations). Andre viewed rewarding students who make conscientious attempts to learn course material as a way to support and encourage students who are struggling with the subject matter.

This strategy may be an effective means for encouraging students to stay involved in complex material, rather than giving up too quickly.

Susan, Marisela, and Rita also described adjusting their assessment priorities, though their approaches differ somewhat from those of Andre and Sharon. Susan and Rita sometimes made use of what Susan refers to as the "fudge factor," "where you kind of make allowances for things that you really can't put a label on, but that you think are present." For example, Susan suggested that she might make allowances for one of her current students, who seem to understand the material as it is presented in class, yet, somehow cannot make the translation in his written work. Similarly, she remarked that she tries to adjust her grading based on the particular and complex life, work, and family situations that students are experiencing. Nevertheless, accommodation is something that she still "kind of agonize[s] over." She stated, "I wish that I had a better way of accounting for people's experiences, or what they bring to class."

Similarly, Marisela varies her course requirements to respond to student needs. If she realizes that a particular method will not work with one of her students, she'll "change things just a hair, and nobody knows any different." Marisela felt that this makes assessment more fair, and less embarrassing, to some students. Rita also recognized that there are often subtle ways that students demonstrate their competence and progress, and she adjusts students' grades, if they are on the line, based on these "general impressions." Although I believe that the similar strategies used by Susan, Marisela, and Rita are more humanistic ways of assessing students, I wonder if students who shy away from connecting with faculty miss out on the benefits of this type of assessment?

Although many of the faculty reported making liberal accommodations to a diverse student body, two of the faculty expressed some reluctance about using diverse assessment methods. Mohammed defended his use of multiple-choice exams for all students, regardless of the diversity of their learning styles and abilities. He had experimented with testing a smaller class twice (once using half short-answer and half multiple-choice questions, and a second time using entirely multiple-choice questions) and found that scores on the first test strongly predicted scores on the second test. Thus, he believed that multiple-choice exams accurately assess the range of performance in his classes. However, he does stress critical thinking (versus rote repetition) in some of his exams. He prefers to use some short-answer questions when possible (i.e., with small classes) because this allows him to get closer to understanding how individual students are thinking about the course material. It seems important to note that Mohammed's desires to foster critical thinking and get to know his students appear to be relatively incompatible with his reliance on multiple-choice exams. Because students are asked to select among possible answers in multiple-choice exams, these exams do not provide many clues about how students are processing class material toward achieving a final answer. Therefore, his opting for multiple-choice exams may reduce Mohammed's ability to understand the way his students are thinking about class material.

David also demonstrated resistance to accommodating diverse students' needs in his laboratory classes. He remarked that the majority of students' grades are based on the final results of their experiments. This strategy does not necessarily take into account students' potential knowledge of the course material but instead places complete emphasis on students' techniques. David's manner of assessment makes me wonder how a teacher establishes a workable balance between assessing student knowledge and assessing student skills?

Soliciting Student Feedback. Four faculty members also agreed on the value of frequently seeking feedback from students. Faculty reported a range of formal and informal methods for assessing both the effectiveness of particular pedagogical strategies and the progress of their students. For example, Susan and Pamela formally and informally conduct course assessments throughout the semester and solicit reflection on individual classes and class activities. Pamela instructed students at the beginning of the semester that she wants them to "be straight" with her as the course progresses, and that, if they face obstacles, they should tell her as they arise, not as the class ends. She found that this tends to discourage them from coming to her after they have already failed the course, when she cannot do much to help them.

Bruce encouraged informal, personal interactions with students, especially when the course addresses sensitive issues. He stated,

> when I'm doing stuff specifically about race and gender, in the hallways, in office hours, and walking back from class, I will take a lot more time to engage students of color in conversation about race or women. It's their section, you know, they're feeling ownership of it (Bruce).

Susan and Sharon required out-of-class office visits to check in with students about their progress and thoughts about the course. Sharon pointed out that strong, personal relationships with her students are a necessary condition for obtaining accurate feedback. Thus, she made a point of getting to know her students and emphasized with them "the importance of their communicating to me early" so she can "find out as early as possible what the issues are." Sharon also allotted 20-25% of students' grades to attendance and participation. She believed that this policy encourages students to come to class and talk, keeping her apprised of their progress.

Nevertheless, two faculty members agreed that soliciting accurate feedback in large classes can be challenging. Sharon suggested that students are more likely to mask their opinions in larger classes, as peer pressure to avoid standing out makes "role playing" more appealing. Mohammed made a similar point, suggesting that monitoring the class's understanding of the material becomes more difficult in large classes because of the reduced level of interaction between faculty and students.

Faculty who addressed the issue of soliciting student feedback may be those who recognize the problematic nature of having one-sided relationships with their students, such as those formed in the banking model of education (Freire, 1970). Instead, these faculty members sought to build more responsive relationships with their students in order to assess students' understanding of course material and find effective ways of presenting course information. Still, I noted that this strategy was mentioned by only four of the ten faculty interviewed. This may imply that soliciting feedback is a difficult strategy for faculty to negotiate. It makes faculty vulnerable to students' criticism and, in the context of larger classes, can highlight a wide array of conflicting feedback that may be overwhelming for faculty to synthesize.

e. Reflections on the Teaching Self

The fifth key theme, which emerged both in the surveys and the interviews, related to faculty's sense of themselves as teachers. This includes faculty's assessment of their "own beliefs and attitudes as derived not only from [their] academic socialization but also from [their] individual experiences of a particular social and cultural background with specific values and belief" (Marchesani and Adams, 1992, p. 13). Faculty's awareness of their own cultural backgrounds can contribute to a better understanding of and interaction with students from diverse populations. These reflections are important to faculty in order to continue and sustain their growth and flexibility as teachers in diverse classrooms.

Five faculty members indicated that they engage in self-reflection to gauge how their teaching impacts their students. Susan continually reflects on the range of student interests and perspectives in her course and the ways that she might take them into account in her teaching. Marisela indicated that she reflects often on teaching students with different learning styles and keeping them all "advancing at the same level." Sharon described making a firm commitment to herself to ensure that students of diverse backgrounds understand the material. She uses this commitment as a yardstick to measure her effectiveness as a teacher in diverse classrooms. Rita commented that she reminds herself to be respectful of students and avoid assuming that everyone shares the same knowledge and experience. In avoiding these assumptions, Rita attempts to bring all students on board at the same level to approach the topic under discussion. She "supplement[s] the background of people who ... aren't at the same level or have a different cultural background."

In contrast to faculty who use self-reflection to set goals for their teaching, Pamela was the sole faculty member who mentioned that her self-reflection led her to see her limitations as a teacher. She feels inadequate at times and worries "that I don't know enough, that I could read from now until ... I'm done with things and just wouldn't feel on top of it enough ... [or] capable of teaching my students what I think would help them." Pamela speculated that her feelings of inadequacy resulted from a lack of graduate-level preparation in teaching and advising students. I agree with Pamela that the lack of formal instructional preparation does put faculty at a disadvantage. This seems particularly true for new faculty members like Pamela. Whereas some faculty may acquire pedagogical expertise over time, others may continue to lack the skills needed to effectively respond to a continually changing student population.

Faculty also reflected on how they monitor themselves in order to encourage a cooperative, open atmosphere where information and experience can be freely and productively exchanged. Susan reflected on her own biases and assumptions, admitting them in order to humanize bias and lead students to their own self-reflection. In a related point, Sharon commented that she encouraged students to be open by presenting herself as approachable and nonjudgmental. She stated, "I have to work really hard at the beginning to make them believe that I'm approachable. They think they're bothering me." Still, Sharon acknowledged that remaining nonjudgmental is not always easy. She stated, "the hardest thing for me is when someone says something that I think is offensive and doesn't know it." Sharon worried, conversely, that certain comments may offend her students and admitted that she sometimes overreacts and makes students uncomfortable. She believed that a more good-natured, but firm, response would be preferable. Sharon raised an important point about the complicated nature of recognizing and respecting diverse students' needs in the classroom. On the one hand, she wants to give space for the articulation of diverse views, and, on the other hand, she is concerned that this allowance may, at the same time, offend some students. Perhaps the balance comes from recognizing and understanding what is offensive without becoming defensive.

Faculty also reflected on their authority in the classroom. Mohammed reflected on his concern that female students view him as "too much of an authority figure," which could lead them to passively accept his teaching and not critically engage with the class material. Having students who view him as the "ultimate expert" may not be in line with Mohammed's previously mentioned goal of encouraging students to think critically.

In contrast to Mohammed, two female faculty of color, Sharon and Marisela, commented that they experience challenges to their authority and view these challenges as linked to racist and sexist behaviors. Marisela noted that both students and fellow faculty continually question her authority. Therefore, it is important to her that she educate people about diversity. Sharon pointed that, because she is a Black woman, students automatically assume that she has an investment in issues surrounding race, and they tend to suspect that she is biased. She considers this a challenge to her authority in the classroom because students often perceive that she places greater value on the perspectives of people of color than on people of White European heritage.

Two White female faculty members also perceived authority as a challenge in the classroom. Susan expressed minor concerns about the threats to her authority associated with talking about her own prejudices in class. While she finds that talking about her "mistakes" regarding prejudice helps to humanizes the issue, she suspects that admitting her own biases detracts from her authority in students' eyes. Rita struggles with the give and take of authority in the classroom in a different way. She circumvents authority issues by modeling a democratic classroom where she and students share authority. The challenge to this approach is that students often do not know how to share authority in the classroom because they have been conditioned into the banking model of education. It is striking that four female faculty reported concerns about maintaining authority in the classroom. This is particularly startling in contrast with the fact that only one male faculty member mentioned authority, and it was in the context of his students granting him too much authority. This contrast seems to illustrate the difference in perceived authority that male and female faculty experience from students in their classrooms.

Subquestion 2: How Do Faculty Think About Course Content in a Diverse Classroom?

Course content refers to the *what* of teaching. The goal of course content is to help students gain a comprehensive and wide-ranging understanding of a given subject. Course content refers to all of faculty's course materials, including their readings, syllabi, and the other resources they use in helping students learn. Faculty responses in both the surveys and the interviews affirmed their understanding of the important role of course content in diverse classrooms. Multiple formatting, student-focused methods, and assessment are integral to how faculty support and inspire students' learning. Yet, developing course content that is representative of many populations, opinions, and ideas is also necessary to engaging and responding to diverse students. This section is divided into two subsections, one addressing readings and resources, and the other detailing how faculty use the syllabus to accommodate diverse classrooms (see Table 16).

Readings and Resources

Most faculty (seven) took into account the representation of authors from varying social identities in their design of course readings and their use of classroom resources. Faculty recognized the importance of bringing in diverse authorships in order to support students' diverse beliefs, values, and social identities and to provide them with an alternative way of looking at the world. Faculty also considered the limitations of the traditional textbook when choosing course materials.

Susan and Pamela both reported that they work to incorporate diverse perspectives in their choices of course readings and materials. Susan attempts to avoid standard, monocultural reading material by creating her own course readers that reflect diverse authors and subject matters. She stated, "I try to use reading packets more than I use textbooks, because that allows me to bring in materials from a number of different perspectives." Likewise, Pamela described incorporating, into each class, empirical work that represents the experiences of various social groups (not just White, middle-class

Table 16 Course Content for Teaching and Learning in Diverse Classrooms

Course Content	Quote
Readings and Resources	"I've made every effort this year ... The readings reflect multiple perspectives, multiple samples, different groups, different ways of thinking about a phenomenon."
Syllabus	"In terms of ... what accommodates diverse needs, what I generally do is to put something in [the syllabus] about how you have to meet with me at some point this semester, regardless of the size of the class, to discuss any fears, concerns, etc., that you have."

families). Pamela also addressed diversity by asking students to help her choose readings that represent various perspectives: "I actually told [my class] at the beginning of the semester that the goal was for them to help me dig up those articles ... and they've got some amazing stuff."

Coretta reported consciously incorporating readings authored by both targets and agents of oppression across eight social identities (race, class, gender, sexual orientation, ability, religion, age, and native tongue). Coretta also ensured that the content of her course readings addresses issues of diversity. She used readings to explore gender, race, class, and religion, stating, "I've made every effort this year ... The readings reflect multiple perspectives, multiple samples, different groups, different ways of thinking about a phenomenon." Coretta even attempted to address oppression on a global level by using readings concerned with language, nationality, and cultural imperialism. Although she has yet to include authors writing on ability, she plans to assign these readings in the future.

In contrast to Coretta, Marisela and Bruce understand the importance of presenting diverse course materials, but both reported using different standards when determining how and to what extent to incorporate these materials. Marisela related that she uses readings addressing diversity only in advanced seminars and when covering specific topics. She does not address all diversity issues in every class because of practical constraints: "I think there's a limit when we're teaching class of what we [can] put across without being too dense ... I would much rather stick to an area and have the students get something out of it than try to pack all the different issues in."

Bruce reported that he tried to ensure some variation in the race and gender of the authors he covers. His readings included some treatment of race and the social construction of Whiteness. Still, he does not intentionally select authors by race or gender — his primary concern is the quality of the writing: "If you've just got all White guys, you're not doing your job ... But, at the same time, I'm not going to focus on that. I want really good articles ... people who engage the students."

Three faculty members stated that they do not concentrate on designing course materials that address diversity. Rita, however, accommodated a range of student abilities in her classroom by paring down the amount of reading she requires a night, from (100 to 150 pages to 15 to 20 pages). She believes that this change has helped students who read slowly and students who have had limited academic preparation. But, whereas this approach is helpful to some students, I wonder how this strategy meets the needs of students who excel and therefore need more of a challenge.

Perhaps faculty can offer supplemental readings in addition to the core requirements, thus satisfying the needs of both groups of students.

David and Andre pointed out that the core readings in their field neglect diversity and that this prohibits them from selecting diverse readings and course materials. David commented that "the syllabus and the reading assignments, they're kind of standard ... You can go to any university in the country and they're teaching the same things in pretty much the same order. It's a very standard course." He also commented that the textbooks focus on the contributions of White males. Andre used almost the same words to make the same point: "I mean, the course catalog says what we're going to cover, and we cover it." Could these faculty members find alternative ways to bring diversity into their readings? From the comments of David and Andre, I found that certain disciplines pose particular challenges because of the lack of access to diverse resources (e.g., guest speakers, videos).

Sharon has experienced the same predicament as David and Andre with regard to the monocultural nature of their available textbooks. However, she compensated for the lack of diversity in her field's literature by incorporating videos and guest speakers into her course. Sharon commented, "I show [videos] and the guest speakers that have come in [are] a way that I compensate in the more mainstream courses. I compensate for the lack of diversity of the literature."

Likewise, both Susan and Marisela mentioned using avenues outside of course readings to introduce diverse perspectives into their courses. Susan used videos to incorporate multiple perspectives. For example, in her conflict and mediation class, she presented videos that do not fit the stereotype of White, middle-class, heterosexual conflict. Similarly, in her course on Central America, she uses videos that reflect national and international perspectives. Marisela brought multiple perspectives into her class discussions by making verbal reference to sources from all over the world. For example, she asked students to examine the different meanings of colors as a function of their cultural context (e.g., white is used for wedding gowns in United States but for mourning in Korea). Marisela stated, "You can have an image but you put it somewhere else and it means something really different."

Regardless of the opportunities that diverse readings and resources offer, Sharon, Bruce, and Pamela suggested that it can be challenging to present a diversity of perspectives when the classroom itself is not diverse. Although Pamela reminded herself to address what the literature omits, such as the African-American experience, the Latino/a experience, and the experience of living in poverty, she admitted that it can be difficult to make omissions salient when diverse voices are not present in the classroom. Despite the difficulty, they are committed to presenting diverse perspectives as a way of preparing students to live and work in a multicultural society. I speculate that this awareness of the increasingly multicultural nature of the world students will face after graduation can be a motivating strategy for other faculty faced with a similar situation.

Syllabus

The course syllabus provides the first opportunity for faculty to state their desired learning outcomes, text readings and materials, schedule, course policies, and course evaluations. Most (eight) faculty discussed constructing their course syllabi in a variety of ways to accommodate diverse classrooms.

Most concretely, Mohammed stated that he takes special care to create a detailed syllabus, so that his students are precisely informed about the course expectations, requirements, and assignments. In the past, he had noticed that students had many uncertainties about his course. Greater detail in the syllabus has helped to relieve this uncertainty. In addition, he intentionally highlights important dates and provides hints for success on the syllabus, which give students a more in-depth picture of his course.

Sharon reported using the syllabus to highlight the centrality of diversity in her course. She commented, "I state really clearly [in the course description] that different groups have different experiences in the economy." Sharon also used the syllabus to convey that students will be expected to describe and explain different groups' current and past experiences in economic structures.

By contrast, Bruce and Marisela demonstrated their commitment to observing students' interests in the classroom by using the syllabus flexibly. Both view the syllabus as a framework from which to work but do not let it rigidly dictate the direction of the course. Bruce begins his treatment of racism by telling students, "We're just going to go until we're done, and I don't know how long it's going to take, and the syllabus goes in the trash can." He commented, "Sometimes it [takes] the rest of the semester ... I think this stuff is too important to, you know, cover the curriculum."

Two faculty members used the syllabus as a way to learn more about their students' diverse needs and to initiate direct contact with students. Coretta designed a new syllabus every year "with an understanding that there will be some diversity of gender, race, transgender, ability, usually not age, but religion, and so on." Then, on the first day of class, she asks the students to spend some time talking about their identities within the learning environment, modifying her teaching based on what she learns. Susan also encouraged her students to discuss their identities, but in the privacy of her

office hours rather than in class. She used the syllabus to offer them this opportunity. She told students, "You have to meet with me at some point this
semester, regardless of the size of the class, to discuss any fears, concerns,
etc., that you have." Via the syllabus she also invited students to talk to her
about learning disabilities or concerns and to give students the telephone
number for the Learning Disabilities Support Services.

For a majority of faculty in this study, the syllabus was, not only a guide
to the course material, but also a way to initiate communication and connect
with students. The TLDC Project devoted special attention to the construction of the syllabus, giving faculty the skills they needed to create a guide
that is responsive to a diverse group of students.

*Subquestion 3: What Further Support Would Faculty Need to Sustain/
Continue Growth as Educators in Diverse Classrooms?*
In this section, I discuss the findings of my third subquestion, "What further
support would faculty need to sustain/continue growth as educators in diverse classrooms?" A similar question was also posed on the survey and gar-
nered responses comparable to the interview responses (see Table 17).
Although understanding what faculty need for support is an important issue, it not the primary focus of this study.

Institutional Support

a. Departmental and Administrative
Faculty expressed a range of opinions regarding the need for increased institutional support in addressing diversity. Six faculty who commented on this
issue believe that departmental and/or administrative support were lacking.
Sharon argued adamantly that both faculty and administrators need to work
harder at addressing diversity: "I wish it weren't a climate where it's seen by
some of the faculty as a mandate imposed by the administration that inter-
feres with academic freedom." She also mentioned that an appreciation for
diversity can enrich the classroom experience.

Two faculty members, Pamela and Susan, expressed that, whereas they
feel supported by their departments in addressing diversity, administrative
support is lacking. In the strongest argument for increasing administrative
support, Pamela contended that the administration is the critical "missing
piece" in the University's attempts to address diversity. She suggested attack-
ing the problem by hiring a department head who is strongly committed to
diversity: "I think we need a department head who's committed to this issue.
I'm really concerned about this sort of whole upper administration." Susan
argued that the University's emphasis on publication toward earning tenure

Table 17 Further Support Faculty Need to Sustain and Continue Their Growth

Type of Support	Quote
1) Institutional support	
a) Departmental and administrative	"I wish it weren't a climate where it's seen by some of the faculty as a mandate imposed by the administration that interferes with academic freedom."
b) Center for Teaching	"I wouldn't mind seeing the Center for Teaching do some diversity training that focuses on racial identity."
c) Structural issues	"I'm worried about the quality of teaching going down because of maybe increased teaching loads and the reduction of faculty ... This is a problem at the highest level."
d) Resources	"There isn't a budget, or the budget is so extremely limited ... The funds to purchase [instructional] material are in such short supply."
2) Collegial support	
a) Interactions among colleagues	"I'd like to see more of the types of discussions that I had at the beginning of my time here at UMASS ... where I could talk to faculty about teaching."
b) Accountability	"[The department needs] watchdogs ... to keep us honest, to keep us on top of it, to keep us diligent."

detracts from the quality of teaching and that the solution lies in rewarding teaching. She believes that, as long as people are not rewarded for good teaching, teaching will suffer:

> I have tenure now but I think that there's a lot of lip service like every-thing else given to teaching and service on this campus and I just think that until they truly reward teaching. But I think that the bottom line for a lot of our untenured people and you know from my perspective when I was untenured was that if I don't get this stuff published nobody is go-ing to care about how good a teacher I am (Susan).

I agree with Susan and believe that part of the problem lies in the ethos of higher education, which bases tenure decisions primarily on scholarship rather than teaching. If the higher education system valued good teaching practices and implemented structures to evaluate them, then universities would offer more faculty support and make good pedagogical practices a more central part of the tenure process.

Like Susan, Bruce thought that the administration limits the University's support for teaching. He believes that the administration will never give him what he needs, citing that "the University is a racist institution ... and it is sexist" and is concerned primarily with making money. He emphasized that you have to address social justice concerns in education "in spite of the University." Given these constraints, diversity training is considered inessential, or "frosting on the cake." Bruce reported that, because he does get the training he needs from the Center for Teaching, he wants the University simply to trust him and stay out of his way. David agreed with Bruce in this respect, commenting that he wants nothing from the University: he would rather they not "get in the way." Andre alone argued that both his department and the University administration feel strongly about the quality of teaching and support it. He continues: "We're doing well compared to fifteen years ago, when the department didn't really know whether they should even invest in [teacher training]. Things have come a long way."

Why is Andre so much more positive about University support than Pamela, Susan, Bruce, and David? I believe a number of factors could be coming into play. First, perhaps, these faculty members may differ in personality, with Andre more apt to look at the world through "rose-colored glasses." Second, faculty's individual positive or negative past experiences with the administration may shape their perceptions of university support. Third, certain disciplines may receive more administrative support than others. Yet, in the final analysis, an impartial review would make plain the University's role as either part of the problem or part of the solution in the larger quest for social justice.

b. Center for Teaching

Seven faculty expressed that the Center for Teaching (CFT) can play a role in refining their attempts to address diversity in the future. These faculty unanimously expressed positive attitudes toward the CFT, remarking that it both reinforces the importance of good teaching and offers concrete advice on teaching for diverse classrooms. For example, Rita contended that the CFT has stimulated faculty (and especially junior faculty) to think about their teaching. She feels that this attention to teaching has actually changed the classroom atmosphere. "There's actually been a change, a democratization of the classroom."

Similarly, David commented that he thinks CFT staff members are doing a great job, particularly in their role as cheerleaders for quality teaching. For him, the CFT plays a crucial role in instilling an appreciation for teaching at the university. Bruce commented that he goes to the CFT frequently for teaching advice and video analysis of his classroom. For him, the Associate Director of CFT is "like a god." Bruce remarked that CFT has given him valuable feedback to improve his teaching. Likewise, Coretta stressed that the one-on-one support she received at the CFT was especially helpful and that she would like to continue receiving such support. She found it "very useful to have a chance to just reflect, one-on-one, with a colleague who was there to support rather than critique and evaluate."

Marisela, Sharon, and Mohammed all offered concrete suggestions for how the CFT could continue to support faculty. Marisela suggested that the CFT hold seminars specifically focusing on small classes. She stated that small classes call for different skills than large classes; therefore, she would like strategy-planning seminars targeting smaller classes. Like Marisela, Sharon commented that she would like to see the CFT expand its offerings. In particular, she suggested adding diversity training focused on racial identity. Mohammed would have liked to improve his teaching through participation in other courses offered by the CFT but remarked that these courses conflicted with his teaching schedule. He suggested that the CFT either announce meeting times at the beginning of the semester or push the seminars to the evening.

c. Structural Issues

Four interviewees indicated that changes to the way the academy functions, including workload, class size, and the nature of the student body, could either help or hinder faculty efforts in addressing diversity. Susan and Andre agreed that department size could impact the quality of their teaching. Susan commented that the declining numbers of faculty affect her ability to concentrate on teaching. She believes that,

> if we had more faculty members there's less demands on any one of us for advisees, committee work, for, as we get more faculty I think the demands outside of just focusing on teaching will be less (Susan).

Andre's concern was less immediate but equally strong. He worried that budget constraints might, at some point in the future, translate into a drop in the number of department faculty and a consequent increase in teaching load. Andre stated, "I'm worried about the quality of teaching going down because of maybe increased teaching loads and the reduction of faculty ... This is a problem at the highest level."

Mohammed and David both expressed concerns about the effects of structural changes on their teaching. Mohammed argued that teaching in diverse classrooms could be improved through reductions in class size — that teaching to large classes is inherently more difficult than teaching to small classes. Mohammed also suggested that university education could be improved by increasing the amount of contact between students and faculty, or between students and their peers, outside the classroom. To David, increasing student diversity and decreasing bureaucratic inefficiency constituted the most salient issues. For him, bureaucratic issues were particularly frustrating: "The main thing that would help around here is a fluid bureaucracy ... I waste a lot of time dealing with bureaucratic stuff on this campus."

Is the academy changing in ways that are moving toward a more corporate model of education? Is this restructuring of academic life drawing faculty away from teaching as one of their primary responsibilities? Faculty members appear to be overburdened by larger class sizes, increased administrative tasks, and more pressure to publish and solicit grant funding for their departments. How do the realities these faculty members describe contradict the land-grant mission of an institution charged with educating its citizenry and reducing traditional obstacles to success? Further, can we expect interaction and community among faculty to thrive and produce better teaching in diverse classrooms under these structural constraints?

d. Resources

Seven faculty members felt they had good ideas for improving instruction but were unable to find the necessary resources. These faculty members mentioned that increasing resources allocated to teaching would help them put their ideas into practice. Rita suggested that she would appreciate more financial support for classroom equipment, photocopying, and teaching assistants. Similarly, both Andre and Coretta related that they need more money for classroom materials. Coretta contended that, "There isn't a budget, or the budget is so extremely limited. So there may be materials we might see, read about, and say 'This would be great for this class,' but ... the funds to purchase such material [are] in such short supply." Susan, who expressed feeling overwhelmed by the number of projects she's involved in, pointed out that a teaching grant would allow her to devote more time to diversify her course materials.

Three faculty members acknowledged that UMASS Amherst could help address diversity by funding conferences and instructional programs, in addition to more fully funding classroom resources. Marisela remarked that going to a national conference on teaching would be an "amazing" experience and that she would like more opportunities to either go to conferences or get videos of talks outside the university. Coretta regretted that she has not had the time or opportunity to learn about the instructional uses of technology (e.g., putting her course on the Web). Although she acknowledged that UMASS Amherst sponsors a technology program for faculty, she believes that the number of people selected for this program is very small. She welcomed more widely accessible instructional programs in technology, stating

> I know that there's a variety of ways that technology can be used to be helpful with diverse student groups. But I haven't had the time or the opportunity to learn about instructional issues of technology. For instance, I imagine that having my course up on a web page could be very helpful to some students. I haven't had a chance to do that. So, support, assistance around the uses of technology would be something that I would find very helpful. The "teachnology" program I assume does that for faculty but it's a very small program (Coretta).

Collegial Support

a. Interactions among Colleagues

Five of the six female faculty members emphasized the importance of continuing to talk with their colleagues about teaching and learning in diverse classrooms. Faculty agreed that they would appreciate access to more structured forums for exchanging information about teaching. Coretta, in a representative comment, stated the following: "One thing that was very helpful [about the seminar] was having the opportunity to sit down with a group of colleagues and talk about teaching and learning … Outside the TLDC Project, there really aren't a lot of opportunities to do that."

Rita related that she would like help from her colleagues specifically around bringing her teaching skills up to date, commenting: "Since I left graduate school in 1973, there have been a real lot of changes in thinking about teaching techniques, and I just find out about those by chance." She recommended providing instructors with informational sources — even written sources, such as handbooks — on a range of techniques that people have used successfully with a range of student populations. Rita also suggested that model classes, led by experienced instructors, would be helpful. Sharon expressed interest in having more contact with fellow faculty through the use of annual or biannual seminars for instructors.

Although these faculty members overwhelmingly expressed a desire to continue interacting with their colleagues, two instructors pointed out that maintaining contact is not as easy as it may seem. For instance, whereas

Susan said she would like to be involved in more discussions among faculty like those she encountered in the TLDC Project, she also found that, when she did try to initiate discussions about teaching in her department, "the same people always show up, and they're the people that I always talk to anyway." Susan, like Rita, reported wishing that the faculty were more open to sitting in on each other's classes and more open to changing their teaching. Likewise, Pamela related that she hopes to continue talking with colleagues and has, in fact, already begun to schedule meetings. Still, she noted that the resistance of her colleagues makes progress difficult and that she struggles to stay positive when most faculty give up or are uninterested in talking about teaching. In light of this resistance, how do faculty respond to the potential isolation of individualized academic work? Are faculty members so overburdened that interactions with their colleagues regarding teaching are reduced to an inconsequential role in their professional lives?

b. Accountability

Although only Pamela mentioned the concept of using watchdogs to help faculty strategize about teaching in diverse classrooms, I find her idea valuable and worth reporting. Pamela believes that, because her department is all White, faculty members are not strongly committed to educating diverse students. Thus, she suggested hiring consultants — colleagues who have studied diversity — to provide feedback and make suggestions for improving teaching. In her words, the department needs "watchdogs ... to keep us honest, to keep us on top of it, to keep us diligent." I support Pamela's idea, however, I wonder about how it would be received in the academy. How could faculty members be encouraged to see this strategy, not as a limitation of academic freedom or an enforcement of political correctness, but as a way of focusing faculty energies toward the ever-changing and diverse needs of their students?

DISCUSSION

The data gathered from the surveys and the interviews reveal similarities and differences. In this section, I state overall comparisons between the survey and the interview findings. Following this general comparison, I address two assumptions that underlie this study: 1) associations between gender and participants' responses, perhaps as result of gender socialization, and 2) associations between race and participants' responses, perhaps as a result of social identities.

The surveys presented six diversity-related dimensions of teaching (awareness of issues of diversity, knowledge of students' social identities, understanding of diverse learning styles, strategies for actively engaging students in learning, fostering community in the classroom, and integrating diversity/multiple perspectives into the coursework) and asked faculty to rate their perceptions of the importance of these dimensions. Surveyed faculty almost unanimously perceived these diversity-related dimensions as important to their teaching.

Faculty members who were interviewed also confirmed that addressing diversity in their teaching is valuable. All participants expressed that they had reflected on how to teach in diverse classrooms and could, therefore, generate a range of strategies. Recognition of the importance of these diversity dimensions by faculty may indicate an awareness that classrooms are increasingly populated by diverse students who have different learning needs and require different pedagogical strategies for success. Faculty members not only recognized the ways in which classrooms are diversifying but also seemed committed to education that meets the needs of all students. Faculty's commitment to educating all students may have been reinforced by the TLDC Project, which emphasized the importance of the six diversity dimensions by presenting them in seminar readings (e.g., Marchesani and Adams, 1992) and discussions.

I concur with the TLDC Project that these diversity dimensions of teaching are important. They represent the multiple aspects that need to be considered when teaching in diverse classrooms. To explore these dimensions in greater detail, an open-ended question on the survey inquired about strategies faculty use for teaching in diverse classrooms (see Table 11). This question generated several overarching themes that clearly emerged, as well, in faculty interviews, including student-focused methods, multiple methods, the teaching self, and course readings. The reemergence of these themes in the interviews confirms both the validity of the categorization scheme used for the surveys and the centrality of these strategies to faculty in their teaching. Faculty may have stressed these themes because the TLDC Project also emphasized these aspects in the substance of its seminars; however, it may also be that, as faculty have experienced the changing needs of their students, they have discovered that these pedagogical practices and strategies work well.

A final comparison that I draw from these findings concerns faculty's thinking about what steps they would like to take and what support they need to improve their teaching in diverse classrooms. The survey question targeting this issue — "What do you see as your next steps for gaining information and skills about teaching in diverse classrooms?" — evoked faculty responses focused on the personal level. For example, faculty members mentioned improving their teaching through continued reading, revision of course content and pedagogy, continued interaction with colleagues and the CFT, and learning more about their students and themselves as teachers. Based on the survey response, I decided to further explore via the interviews what faculty members needed for their own development as teachers. One specific interview question — "What further support would you need to continue growth as an educator of diverse classrooms?" — was designed specifically for this purpose. I also asked probing questions to examine what faculty members needed in terms of their department, the University at large, the Center for Teaching, and anything else important to their teaching. In contrast to the survey responses, this question elicited interview responses that focused primarily on institutional means of support. In general, faculty mentioned needing departmental and administrative support, financial resources, continued professional-development seminars from the CFT, and continued interaction with colleagues.

Responses to both questions targeted the need for continued support from the CFT and continued interaction with colleagues. Initially, I thought the survey question and the interview questions would stimulate similar responses. I found, however, that faculty responded differently. Perhaps this difference was a result of the difference in the research protocols. One factor that may have contributed to the differing responses was the phrasing of the questions themselves. In addition, the survey, which faculty simply completed and returned by mail, did not allow for in-depth exploration of responses, whereas the probing questions of the interview may have prompted faculty to explore more aspects of the support they needed on the institutional level. I believe, however, that the varying research protocols provided me with a better understanding of what faculty need to teach in diverse classrooms on both the personal and the institutional levels.

As helpful as these responses were in examining what faculty see as their next steps for teaching in diverse classrooms, this subject was not the primary focus of my research. In reviewing my interview protocol, I noted that this topic was not addressed as thoroughly as the section on pedagogical strategies and content, which formed the core of my study.

RELATIONSHIP BETWEEN GENDER AND FACULTY RESPONSES

Both survey and interview findings suggest that faculty agree on the value of addressing diversity. Among the faculty who participated in this study I noticed a pattern, however, that participants of the same gender responded in similar ways. Whether or not this pattern was the direct result of gender cannot be completely discerned. Other factors, such as faculty discipline, faculty rank, and individual temperament, also could have impacted on the pattern of responses. Nevertheless, I thought it important to speculate about the relationship that gender may have had on faculty responses as a result of the pattern that had emerged.

I found that female and male faculty differed somewhat in how they put their concerns into practice in the classroom. Specifically, both the survey and interview findings suggest small differences between women and men in student-focused methods, with women using the strategy more often than men. The interview findings provide the strongest support for gender differences on this dimension because, in every subcategory (interactive learning, integrating student experiences into the classroom, encouraging diverse and unpopular opinions, and student participation in setting the terms of their assignments), women accounted for more of the responses than did men (see Table 18). However, one must use caution in interpreting these results due to the small size of the research sample.

On most of the other dimensions, gender differences were less conclusive. Whereas the survey suggests gender differences in the area of general pedagogy, the interview findings suggest no such differences. By contrast, whereas the survey data show no gender differences in the category of teaching self, the interview findings show women reporting responses in this category more often than men. Finally, with regard to course content, both the survey and interview findings indicate quite small gender differences, where women mentioned content-focused strategies more often than men. For example, the interview data show that women were more likely than men to include multiple perspectives as a part of their readings and resources.

In the interviews, female faculty (five) also recommended increased interaction among colleagues as a way to continue their growth as educators. No male faculty interviewed mentioned this as a strategy for future growth. In contrast, however, the survey showed more male support (two out of three total responses) for continued interaction with colleagues at UMASS Amherst, although more women (two) than men (zero) spoke of the need for interaction with colleagues outside of the University campus. These findings demonstrated that female faculty, more than their male counterparts, advocate for increased communication and connection among colleagues.

Meanwhile, two themes emerging solely from the interviews revealed striking gender differences. In particular, more women than men mentioned strategies for fostering community in their classrooms. For instance, women

Table 18 Interview Responses Categorized by Gender

Strategy	Total Mentioned in Section	Female Responses	Male Responses
Pedagogy			
Student-focused Methods	10	6	4
Interactive learning	8	5	3
Integrating student experiences into the classroom	5	4	1
Encouraging diverse & unpopular opinions	2	0	2
Students setting terms of assignments	6	4	2
Multiple Methods	7	4	3
Fostering a Learning Community	10	6	4
Group work	8	6	2
Student disclosure	7	3	4
Assessment	10	6	4
Student-focused	9	6	3
Soliciting student feedback	5	3	2
Teaching Self	6	5	1
Course Content	10	6	4
Readings & Resources	9	6	3
Syllabus	8	4	4

reported using group-work strategies more often than men in order to help students support and learn from one another. Women were also more likely than men to report amending their assessment strategies in order to meet the needs and abilities of diverse students.

Taken together, the findings support the view that women seemed more likely to engage in student-focused methods, fostering community, and student-focused assessment and may suggest that female faculty focus more than male faculty on the interpersonal aspects of teaching. That is, female faculty members focus disproportionately on strategies that create and nurture constructive, interrelational bonds between faculty, students, and the course material.

I believe that gender socialization has had an impact on the aim and ability of some female faculty members to engage with students' experiences. The findings from this research support the idea that socially constructed gender roles may affect the willingness and preparation of faculty to relate to their students in ways that encourage the incorporation of students' experiences in the classroom. In U.S. culture, many women are socialized to place high priority on building and maintaining relationships, providing care and empathy to others, avoiding competition and engaging in cooperation, and creating social networks rather than acting individually. In general, female faculty may be more at ease in working with and finding relevance in students' experiences in the classroom.

It is also possible that students expect female faculty, more than male faculty, to nurture them and acknowledge their experiences. In the United States, women retain the primary responsibility for caregiving. When students enter higher education, they may instinctively transpose these expectations of women onto their female faculty.

Still, it may instead be the case that more female than male faculty are involved in academic disciplines, such as the Humanities and Fine Arts, that readily encourage the integration of student knowledge into their curricula.

CONCLUSIONS

I began this study with the desire to discover what strategies and techniques faculty in higher education use to address their increasingly diverse classrooms. I wanted to address this question to teachers who were experienced and proficient with teaching diverse students, teachers who, by necessity, would have been actively engaged with this question in their professional lives. Faculty who had participated in the TLDC Project were doing exactly this kind of introspective thinking about their own teaching and the means they use to educate a diverse student body.

Several salient pieces of information emerged from faculty who were surveyed and interviewed in this study. First, faculty unanimously acknowledged the importance of diversity in their teaching. Second, faculty explored and used a variety of strategies in order to work effectively with diverse students in their classes. Some prominent themes emerging in both the survey and interview data include the use of student-focused methods, multiple methods, and general strategies, the development of course content, and reflections on teaching self, all in the context of the diverse classroom.

There were, however, some noticeable differences between themes emerging in the surveys and the interviews. During the interviews, faculty brought forth additional strategies they employ in diverse classrooms, including fostering community and student-focused assessment methods. Another theme that emerged was the role of small versus large classrooms. Faculty mentioned that large classrooms can hinder integrating student experiences into the classroom, soliciting student feedback, encouraging diverse and unpopular opinions, and using student-focused assessment methods. It was also stated that teaching in diverse classrooms could be improved through a reduction in class size. These responses demonstrated faculty's energetic, exploratory, and reflective approach towards their teaching to diverse classrooms.

By exploring faculty's definitions of diversity, the interviews clearly highlighted that faculty are actively thinking about issues of gender, race, and class. Faculty demonstrated that they consider these factors both when it comes to tailoring their teaching to diverse students groups and when diversifying course materials. In contrast, ability, sexual orientation, and religion were infrequently the focus of faculty's efforts to address diversity in their teaching. Some faculty cited lack of familiarity and comfort with bringing these identities to the forefront in their courses.

It was also striking that faculty's own gender appeared to play a role in shaping pedagogical strategies for teaching diverse students. The findings suggested that women were more comfortable with developing interpersonal relationships with students, with incorporating student knowledge into the curriculum, and with fostering community with and among students. Assumptions about the effects that racial identity might have on faculty's responses were not confirmed. The findings from the survey demonstrated no concrete distinction between the responses of faculty of color and faculty of White European heritage. The survey data did not represent a large enough sample of faculty of color from which to draw reliable conclusions.

What is perhaps most important to stress about the faculty involved in this study is that they were not typical instructors. Rather, they are exemplary faculty who volunteered to participate in the TLDC Project in order to connect with other faculty endeavoring to improve their teaching for diverse students. Whether it was because of the influence of the TLDC Project, their teaching experiences, or their social identities, these faculty members have developed very thoughtful, complex, original ways of addressing different learning styles, identities, and abilities in the classroom. It is also significant that research and publishing are prominently emphasized at Research One institutions like UMASS Amherst, with possibly less emphasis on the value of good teaching. Although there are some supports for good teaching, such as the Center for Teaching, and awards for outstanding teaching in various colleges and departments, the participants in this study stated that they often faced an uphill struggle in having their instruction to diverse students valued and rewarded by the academy. Providing the administrative and structural support and resources faculty mentioned as necessary to continue their growth as instructors in diverse classrooms will be integral to ensuring that they succeed in their quest for the education of all students. I believe they are, again, exemplary faculty members, whose strategies can be considered ideal for improving teaching for diverse students in higher education.

Chapter 6

Discussion and Implications for Future Research

In this chapter, I summarize the results of the study and discuss these results in relationship to the relevant literature reviewed in Chapter 2. In the final section of this chapter, I provide suggestions for future research on teaching and learning in the diverse classrooms in higher education.

Faculty surveyed and interviewed in this study were self-selected participants in the TLDC Project at UMASS Amherst and, as such, were committed to reflecting on diversity in relation to their teaching. In concordance, analysis of this study's survey and interview data regarding faculty's reflections on classroom diversity in higher education revealed that these faculty recognized the importance of diversity as a component of their teaching. In addition to the affirmation of diversity's relevance to faculty's pedagogy, of paramount importance in this study was faculty's identification of specific pedagogical strategies most helpful in teaching to a diverse student population. I have grouped the strategies that faculty described in both the survey and interview data as most useful to addressing the complexity of needs presented in the diverse classroom into the following three categories: multiple methods, student-focused methods, and development of course content. These three categories will be summarized shortly.

First, it is important to describe the prominent differences between the study's survey and the interview data. The interviews allowed for more in-depth exploration of the issues involved in teaching to diverse students. The interviews allowed faculty to discuss pedagogical strategies not included in the survey, such as practices that foster community and student-focused assessment methods. Another difference that emerged between surveyed and interviewed participants was that those interviewed mentioned the impact of small versus large class sizes on their teaching. Interviewed faculty overwhelmingly stated that large class sizes hindered their ability to bring student experiences into the classroom, solicit student feedback, encourage diverse and unpopular opinions, and use student-focused assessment methods.

Another finding that emerged from the interviews involved understanding how faculty defined diversity. In my analysis of the data, I found that their definitions varied in levels of complexity, with the more complex definitions involving a greater depth of understanding of the cultural and historical implications of teaching to diverse students. Faculty's definitions of classroom diversity were readily arranged along a continuum that moved from recognition and respect, to contextualization, to justice. Moreover, when interviewed faculty discussed tailoring their teaching to and diversifying their curriculum for diverse classrooms, they most often highlighted the social identities of gender, race, and class. Ability, sexual orientation, and religion were less often the focus of faculty's efforts.

Regarding the role of faculty's own social group memberships in the classroom, gender appeared to play some part in shaping pedagogical strategies. Female faculty more often discussed strategies that developed interpersonal relationships with students, incorporated student knowledge into the curriculum, and fostered community with and among students.

An underlying assumption of this study was that both faculty's race and gender significantly influenced their pedagogical practices. However, no relationship could be established, as this study was not designed specifically to investigate the influence of race on teaching practices that faculty used in diverse classrooms. The survey findings did not demonstrate clear distinctions between the responses of faculty of color and faculty of White European heritage.

DISCUSSION OF SELECTED FINDINGS

Monocultural to Multicultural Teaching Practices

Much energy has gone into detailing the reasons that exclusive/monocultural classroom practices fail to meet the needs of diverse students (Banks, 1991; Marchesani & Adams, 1992; Adams, 1992; Chesler, 1996; Kitano, 1997b; Gay, 1997). In addition, multicultural educators, such as Banks (1991) and Chesler (as cited in Schultz, 1992), Marchesani & Adams (1992), Kitano (1997b), have helped to conceptualize the course transformations that need to take place in order to meet the needs of diverse students. As noted in Chapter 2, of particular usefulness to this discussion are the models of Kitano (1997b) and Chesler (as cited in Schultz, 1992), who identify three similar, overarching stages that faculty progress through when changing their teaching. Kitano's stages move from exclusive, through inclusive, to transformed, Chesler's from monocultural, through transitional, to multicultural. Together, their pedagogical models demonstrate the process of change as it moves from exclusive/monocultural teaching to inclusive/transitional teaching, to transformed/multicultural teaching.

To review, Kitano's (1997b) and Chesler's (cited in Schultz, 1992) characterization at the exclusive/monocultural stage of teaching involves faculty who are the sole conveyers of classroom knowledge and who represent and maintain traditional teaching practices. At the inclusive/transitional stage of teaching, faculty remain the primary conveyors of knowledge; however, they use alternative teaching practices to reach students with different learning styles and backgrounds. Building upon the middle stage of inclusive/transitional teaching, at the transformed/multicultural stage faculty and students are co-constructors of knowledge in the classroom.

Particularly because the faculty members in this study were already committed to meeting the needs of diverse students, this study did not seek to compare exclusive/monocultural teaching to transformed/multicultural teaching. Instead, these faculty's experiences helped bring to light the complexities of teaching in the realm that is neither exclusive/monocultural nor completely transformed/multicultural. The faculty members involved in the study were engaged in the process of change, moving away from monocultural models and towards more multicultural models for teaching to diverse students. Their teaching practices did not fall cleanly into one end or the other of the spectrum and are, therefore, within the inclusive/transitional teaching stage of Kitano's and Chesler's models.

No faculty members involved in this study described pedagogical practices typical of the exclusive/monocultural stage of teaching wherein the instructor is the sole conveyer of information who relies on such didactic practices as lecturing and memorization. When their classroom format consisted primarily of lectures, these faculty members reported that student attendance actually dropped and students failed to become invested in the course material. Some faculty recognized, however, that students often have been socialized throughout their school experiences to expect the lecture format. The findings of this study show that lectures were a primary teaching tool that the surveyed and interviewed faculty employed. But lectures were only one among multiple teaching strategies they used to engage students with classroom material and to promote an inclusive atmosphere in which to discuss and question students' understanding of course content.

The important contribution of this study to understanding transformed pedagogical practices lies, therefore, in its offering of a detailed description of the concrete practices that exemplify the inclusive/transitional stage of teaching and in its insight into what supports help faculty make change. One of the most important characteristics of the inclusive/transitional stage of teaching is that faculty play a more dialectical role, in that they remain the primary conveyers of knowledge but, at the same time, attempt to present knowledge in alternative and multiple ways. Findings in this study regarding fostering community, student-focused assessment, and reflections on the teaching self were important. However, multiple methods, student-focused methods, and development of course content were the three most significant faculty teaching practices that emerged from analysis of the study's findings, and they can be used to further elaborate on the inclusive/transitional stage posited in the literature by Kitano and Chesler.

Multiple methods: A majority of faculty in this study acknowledged the importance of multiple teaching methods in their lesson planning process. In their lessons, faculty used a wide range of methods, such as lectures, small- and large-group discussions, worksheets, and multimedia, in order to reach a maximum number of diverse student learning styles and backgrounds. Sharon summarized this approach to teaching when she stated, "I don't think that one set of practices works well for everybody, so I think that you have to use different methods." Further, Pamela stressed that "[I use] as many different teaching styles as I can try because ... people just have different learning styles."

Student-focused methods: In this study, a second way that faculty's pedagogical practices elaborated on the inclusive/transitional stage was in their attempts to engage students in the learning process. To this end, all faculty in the study employed student-focused methods (that is, interactive learning strategies). For example, David and Andre created a more interactive classroom environment through the use of technology. David acknowledged that the answers his students needed to achieve were standardized, yet he has found it important to provide them with the tools by which they could come to the answers on their own, rather than simply giving them the answers. Both David and Andre felt that their use of technology truly engaged students, particularly in comparison with what they viewed as the failures of a traditional lecture format in sustaining active student attendance and attention.

Development of course content: A third way that faculty demonstrated inclusive/transitional teaching was in their encouragement of student interaction with classroom knowledge and their emphasis on peer learning. For instance, Sharon asked students to participate in a game of Jeopardy! in which they studied different social groups and developed questions relevant to these groups. Students were then responsible for posing questions to their peers. Rather than the traditional banking model of teaching (Freire, 1970), wherein the instructor disseminates information to the students, Sharon assigned areas of information. The students themselves researched the course topics and developed relevant questions and answers that they felt would be useful toward a greater understanding of the topics for their peers.

Most faculty in this study used teaching practices that are characterized by Kitano (1997b) and Chesler (cited in Schultz, 1992) as illustrative of the inclusive/transitional stage of teaching. Thus the question arises: what factors may have enabled faculty to develop inclusive/transitional teaching practices?

Importantly, faculty in the study may have had prior investment in exploring alternatives to exclusionary, monocultural teaching. Their experiences in the TLDC Project provided them with a theoretical base, tools, and coaching towards developing more inclusive teaching methods. Further, these UMASS faculty were employed at an institution with an articulated and action-oriented commitment to breaking down educational barriers. Additionally, it is difficult to ignore the rapidly changing character of the student populations in higher education classrooms. Faculty's pedagogical practices reflect ongoing thinking about how to adapt to multiple and changing needs. This kind of thinking may also be done out of necessity; it has become increasingly apparent that monocultural teaching methods may not even serve the needs of the traditional student, defined as White, male, and middle class (Green, 1989). Rather than envisioning one model of teaching and relying on limited and traditional teaching practices, faculty who use inclusive practices take into consideration a multiplicity of student learning styles and experiences.

Faculty may have had additional reasons for moving toward the inclusive/transitional stage of teaching, which emphasizes learning through the use and integration of multiple methods and activities. Faculty in the study found that incorporating and combining elements such as lectures, group discussions, and interactive games, activities, and technologies helped them to avoid student boredom and disengagement. Varying the learning format in these ways also allowed faculty more mobility in the classroom, gaining them greater access to knowledge about how students were responding to and processing course material. Finally, varied formatting often increased faculty's own engagement with the material they were presenting.

The TLDC Project's goal was to encourage faculty to use multiple methods of presenting and analyzing course material. The Project's course readings, including Andersen and Adams (1992), emphasized the importance of varied teaching methods as one effective and immediate tool for improving teaching to diverse students. This emphasis may have encouraged faculty subsequently engaged in this study to begin using multiple methods and to move their teaching toward the inclusive/transitional stage. Additionally, faculty may have been more apt to utilize varied formatting because this technique does not necessitate that they abandon more familiar teaching practices.

Variable formatting provides a guide for faculty to expand their options when planning and designing their courses. Since many faculty members in this study have large classes, multiple formatting provides a way for faculty members to engage more effectively with and meet the needs of large numbers of students at one time. These inclusive/transitional teaching practices can accommodate different learning styles without jeopardizing faculty members' ability to direct and keep order among large numbers of students. Faculty members in this study demonstrated that, although they were invested in multiple formatting, they still played significant roles as the primary conveyers of information in the classroom.

Whereas several potential motivating forces may help faculty to develop inclusive/transitional teaching practices, there are also several counter-forces working against faculty's change efforts toward the end goal of the transformed/multicultural teaching articulated by Kitano (1997b) and Chesler (as cited in Schultz, 1992). Faculty pointed to class size and academic discipline as potential barriers to making progress toward the goal of transformed/multicultural teaching. Interviewed faculty most able to demonstrate transformed elements of pedagogical practices in this study were those who taught smaller numbers of students. Faculty believed that large classes made it difficult to get to know students. Also large class sizes often meant that faculty members were preoccupied with keeping order and managing classroom activities. Those who taught large classes felt they had more difficulty bringing students' experiences into the classroom, helping students to analyze their experiences, and enabling students to take leadership roles in co-constructing courses. These activities require significant time to develop, and faculty in this study may have had insufficient time to cover the course content, as well as to develop student participation skills needed for co-constructing classroom materials.

In addition, faculty's academic discipline may have affected their ability to incorporate elements of transformed teaching. Although faculty discipline could not be discussed in this study because of the requirement to preserve participant confidentiality, faculty interviews indicated the potential effects that academic discipline could have on pedagogy. Some faculty believed that their course content made it difficult to incorporate aspects of transformed/multicultural teaching. Still, the work of Rosenthal (1997), Armendariz & Hasty (1997), Bartlett & Feiner (1997), Donath (1997), and Crow (1997), all of whom address the implementation of multicultural teaching in a variety of academic disciplines, provides hope that transformed/multicultural teaching can be applied in different academic disciplines.

In one example, Rosenthal relates how incorporating aspects of transformed/multicultural teaching into a science course might only require that instructors "increase their awareness of how culture affects science and ... rethink the traditional curriculum and to seek our alternative examples, materials, assignments, and methods of instruction" (1997, p. 149). Rosenthal (1997) offers specific insight into how to teach an introductory chemistry course using transformed/multicultural teaching practices. For example, in a lesson involving units of measurement and interconversions, students from the United States and those from abroad could compare the different systems in various countries and create their own conversions. The authors mentioned above provide rich examples of how vastly different academic disciplines are able to transform their curricula to support diverse students.

Finally, student socialization also impacted faculty's abilities to transform their teaching practices toward the transformed/multicultural stage. Some faculty found that their students were not prepared to engage with the alternative structure of the transformed/multicultural classroom. Overall, only a few faculty in this study described utilizing aspects of transformed/multicultural teaching, and several of them expressed frustration at the resistance of their students to the classroom experience of this teaching practice.

Examining the changes faculty in this study were able to enact, because of constructive factors like their participation in the TLDC Project and their personal commitments, provides compelling evidence to suggest that the process of changing from monocultural to multicultural teaching practices can be successful with appropriate support. Additionally, it may be useful to note that factors such as one's academic discipline or departmental affiliation may even affect one's predisposition to engage with such programs as the TLDC Project and commitments to teaching for diverse classrooms.

The obstacles to further course change are critical to address if the transformed/multicultural classroom continues to be a viable goal for faculty teaching in diverse classrooms. If, as stated by Adams (1992) in Chapter 2, faculty participation is crucial to pedagogical and curricular course transformation, the obstacles to faculty's full participation will need to be more carefully examined.

Monocultural to Multicultural Course Content

Transformation of pedagogical methods is only one aspect of total course transformation that faculty may consider when teaching to diverse classrooms. As discussed in Chapter 2, curriculum refers to the "what" of teaching (Adams, 1992) as opposed to the pedagogical "how." Again, it is useful to compare the faculty experiences in this study with Kitano's (1997b) and Chesler's (as cited in Schultz, 1992) stages of course content change, moving from exclusive/monocultural teaching to inclusive/transitional teaching, to transformed/multicultural teaching.

As Kitano (1997b) and Chesler (as cited in Schultz, 1992) explain, the course content and materials in the exclusive/monocultural classroom support and confirm traditional, mainstream experiences and perspectives. In the inclusive/transitional classroom, course content and materials take an additive approach (Banks, 1997) through the incorporation of diverse experiences and perspectives. At the transformed/multicultural stage of course content, material is presented through the lens of underrepresented perspectives and is used to critically examine individual, cultural, and institutional sites of power and privilege.

In contrast to most faculty members' teaching practices that were largely demonstrative of teaching at the inclusive/transitional stage, there were only a few faculty members whose course contents were characteristic of the monocultural curriculum stage. Specifically, David, Mohammed, and Andre discussed the difficulties they faced in changing their curriculum because of the constitution of knowledge in their academic fields. David explained that the central resources (i.e., course textbooks) that are available for him to work with are based on a standardized model that is used worldwide. These faculty members noticed that, overall, discussions of diversity were not included in their standardized course materials and readings, thus offering little help in diversifying their subject matter.

Notably, particular academic disciplines appeared to lend themselves more easily to discussions of social issues and identities within the course content. The social sciences and humanities, in particular, specifically address human interactions in social, political, and historical contexts and so may be well-suited for the inclusion of such themes in classroom discussions. On the other hand, the natural sciences and mathematics focus more on quantitative rather than qualitative matter and so pose special challenges to faculty's integration of social, political, and historical issues that are intrinsic to issues of diversity in the classroom. In light of the challenges faced in disciplines with standardized course content, which may require specialized analysis to restructure, faculty's concentration on diversifying instructional practices can compensate for what may not be currently available in the area of content.

As in the case of pedagogical practices, the majority of the interviewed faculty demonstrated the development of course content at the inclusive/transitional stage. As Kitano (1997b) and Chesler (as cited in Schultz, 192) indicate, this stage is marked by an additive approach, in which alternative sources and viewpoints are integrated into course content and the prior exclusion of these materials is investigated. Most faculty members were attentive to diversifying their course content to include the representation of authors across a variety of social identities. Specifically, Susan, Pamela, Coretta, and Bruce have all produced their own course readers, enabling them to reflect diverse authorship in their academic field. Several faculty members, including Susan, Sharon, and Marisela, used videos, guest speakers, and verbal references to supplement course content with diverse ideas and perspectives.

Many faculty members were successful at integrating diverse voices into their course content, though particular social identities proved easier or more likely for faculty to incorporate than others. Faculty members were frequently able to introduce content regarding race and gender into their courses. Content about other social identities, such as sexual orientation and class, were incorporated to a lesser degree. Sexual orientation and class are topics that some faculty may feel uncomfortable highlighting in their course content, whereas others may believe these are subjects best left out of academic discussions. Ability and religion were seldom aspects of the course material used by faculty in this study.

Faculty may be more reluctant to introduce content regarding ability because work by people with disabilities has been marginalized and faculty may not have received exposure to the relevant literature. In practice, academic culture has more broadly regarded discriminations of race and gender as relevant subjects of study for a longer period of time. Ability continues to be peripheral in this dialogue. Religious topics inspire similar reluctance in faculty, possibly because discussions of religious diversity can be contentious and can make faculty uncomfortable, in the context of the legal division between matters of church and state in the United States.

Within the inclusive/transitional stage of course content development, there are particular aspects that may create a more hospitable environment for faculty involved in the change process. For example, this approach does not require a comprehensive change in perspective or worldview. Adding diverse content may cause less anxiety for faculty who worry about having to re-learn the contours of their subject matter entirely. However, investigating new materials for a course can be interesting and intellectually stimulating for both faculty and their students, which ultimately can effect a more dynamic learning environment. For faculty members who have been struggling to diversify their course content, the inclusive/transitional approach may produce a tangible result with relative ease.

Many faculty members were engaged in developing course content that included diverse perspectives; however, fewer were involved in what Kitano (1997b) and Chesler (cited in Schultz, 1992) refer to as transformed/multicultural course content. This approach to course content represents a paradigmatic shift, making a concern for multiculturalism paramount and a balance of dominant and nondominant perspectives in the classroom the goal. A few faculty members in this study engaged with this stage of teaching practices. Coretta consciously juxtaposed readings from both dominant and nondominant groups across many different social identities. Coretta, Bruce, and Pamela addressed issues of justice in their course content, framing them under the construct of oppression.

Whereas the inclusive/transitional stage of course content change may be more accessible for faculty, potential obstacles to achieving the transformed/multicultural stage surfaced in faculty interviews. Fewer faculty members have moved into the realm of transformed/multicultural course content, in part, because it requires significant time to identify and review alternative resources. Faculty can be overwhelmed by or resistant to changing their course content and materials when they are already experiencing the pressures of research and scholarship. Faculty's academic disciplines may also present barriers to transforming course content. Some academic fields have not diversified their content and continue to operate according to traditional, monocultural paradigms. Likewise, faculty in positions of social and cultural privilege — Whites and men, for example — may experience difficulty viewing course content through the lens of disempowered groups. A final potential factor restricting faculty from transforming their classroom is a concern for the impact of nontraditional teaching on personnel actions such as tenure, promotion, student evaluations, and merit.

Adams (1992) suggests that many faculty feel more at ease with transforming their curriculum, the "what" of teaching, but struggle with changing their pedagogical practices, the "how" of teaching, to address diverse students' needs. Adams (1992) states that faculty may have more direct control over changing their curriculum and may encounter more success in this area. But the faculty surveys and interviews in this study reveal the opposite view, in which most faculty members described greater ease in transforming their pedagogical strategies. In part, this may be due to faculty's participation in the TLDC Project. The TLDC Project emphasized tools for improving pedagogy and helped faculty to experiment with their practices in the classroom. Faculty see themselves as experts in their curriculum; therefore, transformation in this realm may require expertise that is specific only to those in their own discipline. Faculty's apparent ease with pedagogical change over course content change may also be occasioned by a focus on the practicalities of teaching or by the immediate feedback that faculty may receive when implementing new pedagogical strategies in the classroom.

In relation to faculty's experiences with pedagogical transformation, and in contrast to Adams (1992), the issue of course content change seemed more challenging for faculty in this study. This contrast raises several questions. Why did faculty find it easier to change their pedagogy over their course content? Was there more support from students, administrators, and/ or departmental colleagues for pedagogical change rather than course-content change? Is contemplation of new pedagogical strategies of greater interest to faculty because pedagogical development was most likely not a predominant feature of their graduate training? These questions will be important to explore, particularly if more evidence arises suggesting that pedagogical transformation occurs with greater ease and frequency for faculty than does course content transformation.

Social Group Membership and Faculty Practices

Various authors (Henry, 1993-4; Weiler, 1988; Milem, 1999) assert that the social group memberships of faculty contributed toward the shaping of pedagogical practices. In particular, Milem (1999) noted that female faculty were more likely than male faculty to use active teaching methods (e.g., experiential discussions, cooperative learning, group projects, and student presentations). Analysis of faculty responses in this study revealed similar findings. In this study, female faculty utilized student-focused teaching methods, including active learning, bringing students' experiences into the classroom, fostering community in the classroom through group work, and student disclosure, more often than their male colleagues. These findings supported Milem's (1999) observation that there is a relationship between the gender of faculty and the teaching practices faculty utilize.

Studies conducted by Milem (1999) and Milem and Wakai (1996, as cited in Milem, 1999) also found that faculty of color (African Americans, American Indians, Mexican Americans, Puerto Ricans, and other Latino/as) were likelier to utilize more active teaching methods than White or Asian-American faculty. Milem and Wakai found that the race and gender of faculty were salient factors in determining the likelihood that faculty would use student-focused methods in the classroom.

Although this study did not reveal notable connections between faculty race/ethnicity and the use of particular teaching methods, both gender and race did emerge in important ways in faculty's reflections on their teaching selves. Several teachers writing about their experiences in the classroom, including Bell, Washington, Weinstein, and Love (1997), Rakow (1991), Rhoades (1991), Henry (1993-4), Goodwin, Genishi, Asher, and Woo (1995), and Weiler (1988), stated that their social group memberships led to challenges to their authority in the classroom. These challenges surfaced in the form of students doubting faculty's knowledge of the material, faculty's competence as instructors, and faculty's objectivity in presenting course material. Some writers (Bell, Washington, Weinstein and Love, 1997) also mentioned the risky nature of making personal disclosures in the classroom.

In this study, female faculty of color and White female faculty revealed similar concerns. Several female faculty of color mentioned challenges to their authority in the classroom that could be linked to their gender and race, such as students questioning their knowledge and expertise as instructors and accusing them of promoting their own agendas. Several White female faculty in this study also confirmed challenges to their authority that arose when they disclosed their own experiences and when they attempted to create a more democratic classroom.

These experiences of White female faculty and female faculty of color in this study comprise an approach to teaching in which critical examination and understanding of the teaching self plays a galvanizing role. These faculty members often highlighted perceived tensions among themselves, their identities, and their students, yet they generally utilized examination of the teaching self to improve their teaching. Using a dialectical approach, faculty who engage in thoughtful self-examination can often formulate appropriate responses to their students' needs in the classroom. In one example from this study, a female faculty member noticed that she often overreacted when students made biased comments. Through self-reflection, she developed a calmer, more thoughtful response for the future.

In light of the research of Milem (1999) and Milem and Wakai (1996, as cited in Milem 1999), combined with the findings of this study and the personal accounts of faculty reviewed above, it appears that faculty's social group memberships do impact their teaching and that knowledge of this impact is essential to improving teaching. In this way, faculty reflection on the teaching self functions as a classroom navigational tool, allowing faculty to monitor student reactions, reassess methods, and continually revise their approaches to teaching in order to best meet diverse students' needs. Weiler summarizes this approach when she suggests the importance of addressing students and instructors as "multi-layered subjects" and recommends that both students and instructors should respect and critically examine these layers (1998, p. 126).

Further Support for Teaching in Diverse Classrooms

Faculty who participated in this study discussed the supports they needed to continue their growth in teaching to diverse classrooms. In Chapter 3, I enunciated the commitment of the UMASS Amherst to diversity as stated by former Chancellor David Scott, who has charged the university with educating its citizenry and reducing traditional obstacles "between different groups — faculty, students, staff, and administrators ... between administrative structures, the organization of the University and the physical structures" (UMASS Amherst, Office of the Chancellor 1997-2001). Faculty noted, however, that this commitment to diversity, in and of itself, was not enough to provide support adequate to the task of developing pedagogical and curricular strategies for effective teaching in diverse classrooms.

In their responses, some faculty focused on needing supports at the institutional level, whereas others focused on supports at the personal (classroom) level to help their continued growth as teachers in diverse classrooms. Overall, interviewed faculty acknowledged needing departmental and administrative support, financial resources, continued professional-development seminars from the University's Center for Teaching, and continued interaction with colleagues. They stated that, although the university has taken steps to reward good teaching, such as establishing award programs (e.g., Distinguished Teaching Award) and faculty development programs (e.g., the Center for Teaching), certain institutional practices continue to maintain and encourage traditional, monocultural beliefs. For example, faculty mentioned that the tenure process at UMASS Amherst, which emphasizes scholarship, fails to adequately reward good teaching. In so stating, they echo the observation of Bergquist & Phillips (1975) that many universities do not often reward faculty efforts to develop their teaching practices.

My findings have led me to believe that, if we want faculty to develop their teaching in diverse classrooms, we must have the institutional systems and structures set up to support them. This is in agreement with theorists such as Chesler and Crowfoot (1989; 1997). Many of faculty's responses paralleled elements elucidated in the model of organizational change developed by Chesler and Crowfoot. According to Chesler and Crowfoot (1989; 1997), mission, culture, power, structure, and resources are five elements common to all organizations. Faculty in this study affirmed UMASS Amherst's commitment to diversity as integral to its mission but described a culture lacking in rewards for good teaching, as well as a power system, bureaucratic structure, and resource allocation insufficient to support their growth as instructors of diverse student populations.

To remedy the shortcomings faculty noted, they called for such steps as developing a tenure process that supports faculty in developing and maintaining their teaching skills, restructuring academic functions (e.g., decreasing workload, decreasing class size), continuing and increasing diversity among the student body, and providing faculty development programs that seed quality teaching in diverse classrooms. Faculty also discussed the need for allocating more resources to help them obtain better classroom equipment, teaching assistance for large classes, more money for classroom materials, grants to develop better programs, and increased support for faculty development programs such as the TLDC Project, which offers faculty a forum for ongoing interactions with colleagues to discuss beneficial teaching practices.

As cited in Chapter 2, Adams (1992) and Valverde (1998) state that faculty inhabits the central role at the university for educating and preparing diverse students to participate in a multicultural society. In order for faculty to move their classrooms toward the social justice phase of the continuum I have outlined, universities must back up their missions to diversity by providing the institutional supports and structures required for the change needed to support faculty in their commitment to educating students for entrance into an increasingly multicultural world.

IMPLICATIONS FOR FUTURE RESEARCH

The study of classroom diversity in higher education is a subject barely past its infancy. The findings of this study add to the correspondingly sparse literature on this subject. Further study is needed to broaden our understanding of pedagogical practices that are effective in teaching in the diverse classroom. Because most participants in this study had moved from exclusive/monocultural teaching to inclusive/transitional pedagogical and curricular practices, this study has given insight into the concrete practices that faculty are utilizing in the inclusive/transitional stage of teaching to diverse classrooms. However, this study has provided only glimpses of practices in the transformed/multicultural stage. A possible direction for future research may address the range of concrete practices faculty utilize in the transformed/multicultural stage of teaching to diverse classrooms.

Other directions for future study may involve investigating the process that have led faculty to transform their teaching practices and course content. Investigative questions may include the following: How did the faculty in this study arrive at the inclusive/transitional stage? How much of their growth resulted from their own motivation? How much of their growth resulted from supports they received from their departments, development programs, and/or other institutional resources?

Further study may involve the relationship between professional development programs and the transformed classroom. One question raised by this study is: How do faculty members continue to develop their pedagogical practices and course content to move from the inclusive/transitional to the transformed/multicultural stage? For some faculty, this may be a deeply personal, individualistic process (e.g., reading, self-reflection). For others, faculty development programs (e.g., seminars, workshops) may be key in helping them acquire the instructional skills needed to transform their teaching.

Whereas this study explored faculty's perceptions of their teaching, further research may focus on classroom observation as a tool to understanding the impact of pedagogical practices on students, as well as understanding the connections — and possible lack of connections — between faculty perceptions and actual practices. Classroom observation could also plumb an understanding of diverse students' perceptions of faculty practices and their effectiveness, thereby engaging a more holistic picture of the classroom and a deeper examination of effective pedagogical practices for diverse student populations.

Another theme for possible study involves examining the influence of class size on effective teaching practices in diverse classrooms. In this study, faculty frequently mentioned that large class size impeded their ability to connect with diverse students in and outside of the classroom, to engage students in bringing their own experiences into the classroom, and to foster classroom community. How can faculty in large classrooms overcome this impediment in order to achieve multiculturally competent teaching practices? Another area of exploration involves exploring how faculty made progress in large classrooms from the exclusive/monocultural stage to the transformed/multicultural stage of teaching.

The relationship between academic discipline and effective pedagogical strategies/curriculum development should also be explored in future research. Academic disciplines such as natural sciences and mathematics may pose a different challenge to faculty looking for ways to transform their curricula and pedagogical practices. Further studies could examine the similarities and differences among varying academic disciplines to determine strategies for effective teaching in diverse classrooms. What, for example, are the effects of academic discipline on moving from the inclusive/transitional to the transformed/multicultural stage of teaching? What concrete practices are utilized by faculty in the natural sciences and mathematics as part of the transformed/multicultural stage? How do these differ from the practices used in this stage by faculty in the social sciences and humanities?

The academic discipline in which one teaches affects teaching practices in the diverse classroom, yet other variables may also impact teaching, including but not limited to academic discipline, teacher preparation, teaching mentors and role models, and institutional sanctions and rewards for classroom teaching.

Still another area for future study involves examining the influence of faculty's gender, race, and/or other social identities on pedagogical practices and curricula in diverse classrooms. In Chapter 1, I stated a working assumption that the social identities of participants would have an impact on their teaching. This assumption is supported by Sleeter (1992), Rakow (1991) and Milem (1999). However, other data, including Saulter (1996) and the analysis from the interview findings in this study, have called this assumption into question. Further research could explore the relationship between faculty's social identities and the strategies they use in teaching to diverse students. Three possibilities for future study include investigating the experiences of White faculty and faculty of color when teaching to diverse classrooms, the role of social identities in the investment faculty have in developing a multicultural agenda, and the relationship between social identities and the teaching strategies effective for diverse students.

Research into faculty practices at other institutions of higher education could explore the effect of teacher reward systems on faculty's motivation to examine and transform their own pedagogical practices. A possible study might compare the motivation of faculty rewarded for good teaching in their tenure process versus those in the publish-or-perish type of institution that places singular premium on publishing efforts. Such research would lend important insights into the reward systems needed to support faculty in teaching to diverse classrooms. A final area for future study involves the assessment and evaluation of faculty development programs such as the

TLDC Project. This research is important in assessing the impact of teacher development programs on faculty's experiences, pedagogical practices, and curricula to more effectively meet the needs of both faculty and diverse student populations.

I embarked on this study to examine faculty's reflection on their experiences and pedagogical practices of teaching in diverse classrooms. In Chapter 1 of this study, I referenced the observations of Dixon (1997) concerning the responsibility faculty have in establishing pedagogical practices and curricula that encourage the academic success of diverse students. At a Research One university, faculty often faces institutional, structural, and cultural barriers to focusing on teaching and teaching development, in general, and teaching in diverse classrooms, in particular. The UMASS Center for Teaching has made a significant contribution in offering faculty support for teaching in diverse classrooms.

The faculty members who participated in this study are transcending Dixon's appraisal of the current preparedness of higher education faculty. These faculty members understand the importance of diversity and are committed to the multicultural transformation of teaching practices and course content, preparing students to interact in a multicultural community. The faculty members in this study were exemplary and committed in their quest for effective education of diverse student populations in higher education.

In conclusion, as universities become inevitably more diverse, it is important for both individual faculty and the institutions in which they work to support and encourage modes of teaching and learning that expand far beyond monoculturalism. As we recognize the importance of all students learning to live and work in a multicultural society, working toward transformed teaching and learning in diverse classrooms benefits all learners. This study demonstrates that, when provided with institutional support and specific strategies for change, university faculty in multiple disciplines are committed to exploring teaching practices and content with the goal of becoming more effective in diverse classrooms.

APPENDIX A
Pre-Contact via Electronic Mail

Dear _____:

My name is Carmelita (Rosie) Castañeda, and I am a doctoral candidate in the Social Justice Education Program at the University of Massachusetts Amherst. I am undertaking a study that focuses on how faculty who participated in the Teaching and Learning in Diverse Classroom Faculty and TA Partnership (TLDC) Project, reflect on their experiences as instructors in diverse classrooms.

In a few days you will receive a survey that will take approximately 15 minutes to complete. This survey addresses: 1) your experiences with the TLDC Project, 2) your professional development experiences with teaching in diverse classrooms, 3) your experience with teaching in diverse classrooms, and 4) your background. I appreciate your consideration in completing this survey and returning it to me. This study has full support of the Center for Teaching. Your participation will make a significant contribution to our understanding of how faculty make sense of teaching in diverse classrooms and in our understanding of the impact of the TLDC Project. Thank you in advance for your assistance.

Sincerely,

Carmelita (Rosie) Castañeda

APPENDIX B
Survey Cover Letter First Mailing

TEACHING AND LEARNING IN DIVERSE CLASSROOMS SURVEY

My name is Rosie Castañeda, and I am a doctoral candidate in the Social Justice Education Program at the University of Massachusetts Amherst. I am undertaking a study focusing on how faculty who participated in the Teaching and Learning in Diverse Classroom Faculty and TA Partnership (TLDC) Project at UMASS between 1994-2000, reflect on their experiences as instructors in diverse classrooms. This study has the support of the Center for Teaching.

I am contacting you now in the hope that you will agree to respond to the attached survey. This survey will take approximately 10 – 15 minutes to complete, and it is organized in three sections: 1) your experiences with the TLDC Project, 2) your experience with teaching in diverse classrooms, and 3) your background. Following completion of the surveys, I will invite a small number of the faculty to participate in a follow-up interview.

The data collected from this survey will fill a critical research gap, enumerating the methods that faculty use in their teaching practices in diverse settings. Participant's names will not be used. Information from all completed surveys will be reported as a conglomerate so that the answers will remain confidential. The results of this study will be written up as my doctoral dissertation, and may be reproduced for publication in professional journals. You may review the data at any time prior to my final oral defense and/or written publication by contacting me at the phone/email listed below.

If you agree to participate in this study please sign the enclosed informed consent and return it to me at your convenience. Participation in this study is voluntary and your decision to participate or not to participate will in no way incur judgment. You may also withdraw from part of all of this study at any time.

Thank you for your time in responding to this survey. Your participation will make a significant contribution to our understanding of how faculty make sense of teaching in diverse classrooms and in our understanding of the impact of the TLDC Project. If you have any questions please contact me by telephone at (413) 585-8297 or by e-mail at *carmelit@educ.umass.edu.*

Thank you,

Rosie Castañeda, M.S.
Doctoral Candidate Social Justice Education

APPENDIX C

Teaching and Learning in Diverse Classrooms Survey

The purpose of this survey is to collect data focusing on the ways in which faculty, who have completed the Teaching and Learning in Diverse Classroom Faculty and TA Partnership (TLDC) Project, reflect on their experiences as instructors from 1994-2001. Your responses will be reported along with other participants of the TLDC Project. No faculty name will be attached to the survey they submit in order to ensure complete confidentiality. Completing this survey will take approximately 10-15 minutes. Once completed, please return the survey to: Rosie Castañeda, P.O. Box 2052 Amherst, MA 01004. For your convenience, an addressed stamped envelope has been provided.

Thank you for your time in responding to this survey. Your answers are an essential part of understanding how faculty think about teaching in diverse classrooms. Please return the survey by March 15, 2001.

A. The questions in this section concern your experiences with the TLDC Project.

1. Indicate the extent to which each item listed below has been impacted by the TLDC Project:
(N/A – Not Applicable; 1 = Not at all; 2 = To a little extent; 3 = To some extent; 4 = To a great extent)

Your philosophy of teaching   N/A   1   2   3   4
Your awareness about how diversity impacts
  learning   N/A   1   2   3   4
Your knowledge of students' racial/ethnic

background(s)	N/A	1	2	3	4
Your awareness of your own social identities	N/A	1	2	3	4
Your understanding of how students learn	N/A	1	2	3	4
Your strategies to actively engage students in their own learning	N/A	1	2	3	4
Your strategies to foster community in the classroom	N/A	1	2	3	4
Your course design (course description, syllabus)	N/A	1	2	3	4
Your approach to class preparation	N/A	1	2	3	4
Your readings & assignments (homework, in-class)	N/A	1	2	3	4
Your assessment methods (Mid-terms/Final Exams)	N/A	1	2	3	4
Other _____(Please Specify)	N/A	1	2	3	4

2. What motivated you to participate in the TLDC Project?

3. What aspects of the TLDC Project were most helpful to you during your participation in the program. (Circle one)
    (N/A = Not Applicable; 1 = Not at all; 2 = To a little extent; 3 = To some extent; 4 = To a great extent)

Teaching Projects	N/A	1	2	3	4
Group Meetings/Ongoing Seminars	N/A	1	2	3	4
Individual Consultation with TLDC Staff	N/A	1	2	3	4
Mid-semester Assessment	N/A	1	2	3	4
Lending Library/Resources/Bibliography	N/A	1	2	3	4
Work with TA (s)	N/A	1	2	3	4

4. Since you participated in the TLDC Project, to what extent have you had continued interactions with:
    (1 = Not at all; 2 = To a little extent; 3 = To some extent; 4 = To a great extent)

Faculty in your TLDC cohort	1	2	3	4
TLDC participants not in your cohort	1	2	3	4
Center For Teaching Staff at UMASS	1	2	3	4

B. This section focuses on your professional development experiences with teaching in diverse classrooms.

    1.   What courses or professional development seminars addressing diversity had you taken *prior to your participation* in the TLDC Project?

    2.   What courses or professional development seminars addressing diversity in the classroom have you taken *since your participation* in the TLDC Project?

C. This section focuses on your experiences with teaching in diverse classrooms.

    1.   In your own teaching, to what extent are each of the following dimensions effective in teaching in diverse classrooms?
        (N/A = Not Applicable; 1 = Not at all; 2 = To a little extent; 3 = To some extent; 4 = To a great extent)

Awareness of issues of diversity	N/A	1	2	3	4
Knowledge of student's social identities	N/A	1	2	3	4
Understanding diverse learning styles	N/A	1	2	3	4
Strategies for actively engaging students in their learning	N/A	1	2	3	4
Fostering community in the classroom	N/A	1	2	3	4
Integrating diversity/multiple perspectives into coursework	N/A	1	2	3	4

2. Are there any specific teaching strategies that you find to be effective in teaching in diverse classrooms? Please describe below.

3. What do you see as your next steps for gaining knowledge and skills about teaching in diverse classrooms? Please describe below.

D. The questions in this section focus on your personal and professional characteristics.

1. In what school/college at UMASS is your primary faculty appointment?
   _____

2. For how many years have you been a faculty member at UMASS?
   _____

3. What is your current rank? (Circle one)

Professor   Associate Professor   Assistant Professor   Lecturer

4. What is your gender? (Circle one)

        Female   Male   Transgender

5. Which of the following BEST describes your race or ethnicity?: (Circle one)
   Bi-racial or Multi-racial
   Black
   Asian or Pacific Islander
   Latino/a Hispanic
   Native American or Alaskan Native
   White or European American
   Cape Verdean
   Other _____ (Please specify)

Please add any other comments you would like to share about the TLDC Project or your experience with the program.

Please return this survey by March 15, 2001, in the enclosed addressed stamped envelope to: Rosie Castañeda, P.O. Box 2052, Amherst, MA 01004
Thank you for your time

APPENDIX D

Informed Consent Form for Survey

Teaching and Learning in the Diverse Classroom: Faculty Reflections On Their Experiences and Pedagogical Practices of Teaching Diverse Populations.

CONSENT FOR VOLUNTARY PARTICIPATION

My name is Carmelita (Rosie) Castañeda, and I am a doctoral candidate in the Social Justice Education Program at the University of Massachusetts Amherst. I am undertaking a study on how faculty who participated in the Teaching and Learning in Diverse Classroom Faculty and TA Partnership (TLDC) Project, from 1994-2000) at UMASS reflect on their experiences as instructors in diverse classrooms. I greatly appreciate your participation. Please note the following consent protocols below.

I volunteer to participate in this study and understand the following:

1. The questions I will be answering on the survey address my views on issues related to my experience with teaching in diverse class-rooms, my experience with the TLDC Project at the University of Massachusetts Amherst, and my background. I understand that the primary purpose of this research is to describe methods that faculty use in their teaching practices in diverse settings.
2. The survey results will be reported as descriptive statistics facilitated by the use of SPSS: a statistical analysis program.
3. In order to maintain confidentiality, my name will not be used, nor will I be identified personally in any way or at any time.
4. I may withdraw from part or all of this study at any time, and I am free to participate or not to participate without judgment.

5. I have the right to review material prior to the final oral exam or publication of results.
6. I understand that results from this survey will be included in Carmelita (Rosie) Castañeda's doctoral dissertation, and may also be included in manuscripts submitted to professional journals for publication.

_____   _____

Carmelita (Rosie) Castañeda   Date   Participant's Signature   Date
Researcher

APPENDIX E

Reminder Postcard for Survey

Teaching and Learning in Diverse Classrooms Survey

To: Participants in the Teaching and Learning in Diverse Classroom Faculty and TA Partnership Project Survey

This is a friendly reminder about completing the TLDC survey. Your insights and perspectives are critical to understanding teaching in diverse classrooms. Other phases of my research cannot be carried out until I complete analysis of the survey data.

I am grateful that you are taking the time to complete the survey, which will help to further my study. If you have already returned the survey, please accept my thanks and know that your efforts are much appreciated.

Thank you,

Carmelita (Rosie) Castañeda
Doctoral Candidate
Social Justice Education Program

APPENDIX F

Survey Cover Letter Second Mailing

Reminder: Teaching and Learning in Diverse Classrooms Survey

As you may remember, my name is Carmelita (Rosie) Castañeda, and I am a doctoral candidate in the Social Justice Education Program. A few weeks ago I sent you a letter and a survey regarding teaching and learning in the diverse classrooms (TLDC). This is a follow-up letter to request the favor of your response.

The return of your survey means a lot to me as it will not only provide valuable information that I can share with other educators but also it will help me complete my doctoral degree and pursue a career in higher education. Therefore, I am grateful for your willingness to complete the enclosed survey. Please return the survey and your informed consent form by April 6, 2001. Other phases of my research cannot be carried out until I complete analysis of the survey data. This study has the support of the Center for Teaching.

The data collected from this survey will fill a critical research gap enumerating the methods that faculty use in their teaching practices in diverse settings. Participants' names will not be used in order to maintain confidentiality. Information from all completed surveys will be reported as descriptive statistics facilitated by the use of SPSS (a statistical analysis program). I will write up the results as my doctoral dissertation, and these findings may be reproduced for publication in professional journals. You may review the data at any time prior to my final oral defense and/or written publication by contacting me at the phone/e-mail listed below.

If you agree to participate in this study, please sign the enclosed informed consent form and return it to me along with your survey. Participation in this study is voluntary, and your decision to participate or not to participate will in no way incur judgment. You may also withdraw from part of or all of this study at any time.

Thank you for your time in responding to this survey. Your participation will make a significant contribution to our understanding of how faculty make sense of teaching in diverse classrooms and in our understanding of the impact of the TLDC Project. If you have any questions, please contact me by telephone at (413) 585-8297 or by e-mail at carmelit@educ.umass.edu.

If you have already returned the survey, please accept my thanks, and know that your efforts are much appreciated.

Thank you,

Carmelita (Rosie) Castañeda
Doctoral Candidate, Social Justice Education Program

APPENDIX G

Guiding Interview Protocol

Introduction:
Hello, my name is Carmelita Castañeda; I am a doctoral candidate in the Social Justice Education Program. As you may remember my doctoral research focuses on how faculty, who participated in the TLDC Project, reflect on their experiences as instructors in diverse classrooms. Based on the results of the surveys I have decided to explore more thoroughly how faculty think about instructional strategies used to teach in diverse classrooms and to explore more thoroughly how faculty think about course content/curriculum when teaching to diverse student groups.

Before we begin the interview I would like to review the interview protocol. (Go over the consent form)

Do you have any questions?

Please sign the consent form.

Background questions:
I will begin the interview by asking you a few background questions.

1. Tell me a little about the courses you are teaching this semester.
2. You have been through the TLDC Project and have shown an interest in diversity. What does diversity mean to you in the classroom context?
3. To the best of your knowledge, in what ways is your classroom a diverse classroom? (gender, race, ability, sexual orientation)

Teaching to diverse classrooms questions:

1. What instructional practices do you think "work" when you teach to diverse classrooms?
2. Can you describe a specific example when the instructional practice you used was *effective* with diverse students in your classroom? What made this an unsuccessful experience?
3. What challenges have you encountered when teaching to diverse student groups?
4. Can you describe a specific example when the instructional practice you used was ineffective with diverse students in your classroom? What made this a successful experience?
5. How have you designed your course content to facilitate success for diverse students? Some of the areas are...

TLDC related question:

Are there ways in which participating in the TLDC Project helped you to make changes in your instructional practices? In terms of devising your course curriculum/content? If so, in what ways? If not, why not?

Further Support question:

What further support would you need to continue growth as an educator of diverse classrooms? In terms of your Department, UMASS at large, The Center for Teaching?

Other?

Wrap-up:

Is there anything else you would like to add about teaching in diverse classrooms?

Do you have any questions for me?

Thank you for your time and willingness to participate in this interview.

APPENDIX H

Electronic Mail Interview Confirmation Letter

Dear_____:

Thanks for agreeing to participate in the interview process that we have arranged for the purpose of gathering additional information regarding faculty reflections of their teaching experiences in diverse classrooms.

We are scheduled to meet on_____.

Below I have listed some of the questions that we will be discussing during the interview. I provide this for you to offer you the opportunity to reflect on these questions before we meet.

I look forward to meeting with you. Thanks again for helping me further my doctoral research.

Sincerely,

Rosie Castañeda

Questions:

Give your definition of diversity.

What instructional practices do you think "work" when teaching in diverse classrooms?

Describe a specific example when the instructional practice you used was effective with diverse students in your classroom? What made this a successful experience?

What challenges have you encountered when teaching to a diverse classroom?

Describe a specific example when the instructional practice you used was ineffective with diverse students in your classroom? What did not work? What could have been done differently?

How have you designed your course content to facilitate success for diverse students? (course syllabus, course description, readings, assignments, assessment, etc.)

Are there ways in which participating in the TLDC Project helped you to make changes in your instructional practices or course content? If so, in what ways? If not, why not?

APPENDIX I

Interview Informed Consent

Teaching and Learning in the Diverse Classroom: Faculty Reflections On their Experiences and Pedagogical Practices of Teaching Diverse Populations

CONSENT FOR VOLUNTARY PARTICIPATION

My name is Rosie Castañeda, and I am a doctoral candidate in the Social Justice Education Program at the University of Massachusetts Amherst. I am undertaking a study of how faculty who participated in the Teaching and Learning in Diverse Classroom Faculty and TA Partnership (TLDC) Project, from 1994-2000 at UMASS-Amherst, reflect on their experiences and pedagogical practices as instructors in diverse classrooms. I greatly appreciate your participation. Please note the following consent protocols below.

I volunteer to participate in this study and understand the following:
   a. I will be interviewed by Rosie Castañeda using a guided interview format consisting of three primary questions.
   b. The questions I will be answering during the interview address my views on issues related to my experience with teaching in diverse classrooms, and my experience with the TLDC Project at the University of Massachusetts Amherst. I understand that the primary purpose of this research is to describe methods that faculty use in their teaching practices in diverse settings.
   c. The interview will be tape recorded and transcribed to facilitate analysis of the data. Pseudonyms will be used in all written reports and presentations.

   d. My name will not be used, nor will I be identified personally in any
       way or at any time.
   e. I may withdraw from part or all of this study at any time and I am
       fee to participate or not to participate without prejudice.
   f. I have the right to review material prior to the final oral exam or
       other publication.
   g. I understand that results from this interview will be included in
       Rosie Castañeda's doctoral dissertation and may also be included
       in manuscripts submitted to professional journals for publication.

_____   _____
Carmelita (Rosie) Castañeda   Date   Participant's Signature   Date

Bibliography

Adams, M. (1992). Cultural inclusion in the American college classroom. *New Directions for Teaching and Learning, 49,* 5-17.

Adams, M. (1997). Pedagogical frameworks for social justice. In M. Adams, L. Bell, & P. Griffin (Eds.), *Teaching for diversity and social justice.* New York: Routledge.

Adams, M., Brigham, P., Dalpes, P., & Marchesani, L. (Eds.). (1994). *Diversity and oppression: Conceptual frameworks.* Dubuque, IA: Kendall/Hunt Publishing.

American Association for Higher Education (AAHE). (1989). *Faculty inventory: Seven principles for good practices in undergraduate education* [pamphlet]. Racine, WI: The Johnson Foundation.

American Council on Education & American Association of University Professors. (2000). *Does diversity make a difference? Three research studies on diversity in college classrooms.* Executive Summary. Washington, D.C.

Andersen, M. (1985). Women's studies/black studies: Learning from our pasts/ forging a common future. In M. Schuster & S. Van Dyne (Eds.), *Women's place in the academy: Transforming the liberal curriculum.* New Jersey: Rowman & Allanheld.

Anderson, J., & Adams, M. (1992, Spring). Acknowledging the learning styles of diverse student populations: Implications for instructional design. *New Directions for Teaching and Learning, 49,* 19-31.

Armendariz, E.P., & Hasty, L. (1997). Making mathematics instruction inclusive. In A. Morey, & M. Kitano, (Eds.). *Multicultural course transformation in higher education.* Boston, MA: Allyn and Bacon Publishers.

Asante, M. (1991). The afrocentric idea in education. *Journal of Negro Education, 60*(2), 170-180.

Ashton, N. (1996). Involving faculty in curriculum transformation: Overcoming resistance at Richard Stockton College. In E. Friedman, W. Kolmar, C. Flint, & P. Rothenberg (Eds.), *Creating an inclusive college curriculum.* New York: Teachers College.

Association of American Colleges and Universities, University of Maryland, & Diversity Connections. (1999, September). The court of public opinion: The Ford Foundation campus diversity initiative survey of voters on diversity in education. *Equity & Excellence in Education, 32,* 17-20.

Au, K., & Jordan, C. (1981). Teaching reading to Hawaiian children: Finding a culturally appropriate solution. In H. Trueba, G. Guthrie, & K. Au (Eds.), *Culture and the bilingual classroom studies in classroom ethnography* (pp. 139-152). MA: Newbury House.

Au, K., & Kawakami, A. (1994). Cultural congruence in instruction. In E. Hollins, J. King, & W. Hayman (Eds.), *Teaching diverse populations: Formulating a knowledge base.* New York: State University of New York.

Ayers, W. (1995). Becoming a teacher. In W. Ayers (Ed.), *To become a teacher: Making a difference in children's lives.* New York: Teachers College.

Babbie, Earl. (1983). *The practice of social research.* Belmont, CA: Wadsworth Publishing.

Bacon, C. (1996). Curriculum transformation for basic English composition and introduction to literature: A review from the trenches. In E. Friedman, W. Kolmar, C. Flint, & P. Rothenberg (Eds.), *Creating an inclusive college curriculum.* New York: Teachers College.

Baldwin, R. G., & Blackburn, R.T. (1981), The academic career as a development process. *Journal of Higher Education, 52*(6), 598-614.

Banks, J. (1991). *Teaching strategies for ethnic studies* (5th ed.). Boston: Allyn and Bacon.

Banks, J. (1995). Multicultural education: Historical development, dimensions, and practice. In J. Banks & C. Banks (Eds.), *Handbook of research on multicultural education.* London: Macmillan.

Banks, J. (1997). Multicultural education: Characteristics and goals. In J.A. Banks & C.A. McGee Banks (Eds.), *Multicultural education: Issues and perspectives* (3rd ed.). Boston: Allyn & Bacon.

Barringer, H. R., Takeuchi, D. T., & Xenos, P. (1995). Education, occupational prestige, and income of Asian Americans. In D. T. Nakanishi & T. Y. Nishida (Eds.), *The Asian American educational experience: A source book for teachers and students.* New York: Routledge. (Original work published 1990).

Bartlett, R.L., & Feiner, S.F. (1997). Integrating race and gender into introductory economics. In A. Morey & M. Kitano (Eds.). *Multicultural course transformation in higher education.* Boston, MA: Allyn and Bacon Publishers.

Beckhard, R., & Pritchard, W. (1992). *Changing the essence: The art of creating and leading fundamental change in organizations.* San Francisco: Jossey-Bass.

Bell, L.A., Washington, S., Weinstein, G., & Love, B. (1997). Knowing ourselves as instructors. In M. Adams, L.A. Bell, & P. Griffin (Eds.). *Teaching for Diversity and Social Justice.* New York: Routledge.

Bennett, C. (1976). Students' race, social class, and academic history as determinants of teacher expectation of student performance. *Journal of Black Psychology, 3*(1), 71-86.

Bennett, C. (1982, Winter). A case for pluralism in the schools. *The Newsletter of the National Association for Multicultural Education, 1*(2), 589-592.

Bennett, C. (1995). *Comprehensive multicultural education: Theory and practice* (3rd ed.). Boston: Allyn & Bacon.

Bergquist, W.H., & Phillips, S.R. (1975). Components of an effective faculty development program. *Journal of Higher Education, 46*(2), 177-215.

Bergquist, W.H., & Phillips, S.R. (1979). *A handbook for faculty development* (Vol. 2). Washington, D.C.: The Council for the Advancement of Small Colleges.

Bess, J. (Ed.). (1997). *Teaching well and liking it: Motivating faculty to teach effectively.* Baltimore, MD: Johns Hopkins UP.

Blackburn, R.T. (1980). *Project for faculty development program evaluation: Final report.* Center for the Study of Higher Education-Michigan University Ann Arbor, MI: (ERIC Document Reproduction Service No. ED 208 767).

Bland, C.J., & Schmitz, C.C. (1988). Faculty vitality on review: Retrospect and prospect. *Journal of Higher Education, 59*(2), 190-224.

Bloom, A. (1987). *The closing of the American mind.* New York: Simon & Schuster.

Bogdan, R., & Biklen, S. (1982). Qualitative research for education: An introduction to theory and methods. Boston, MA: Allyn and Bacon.

Braskamp, L., Fowler, D., & Ory, J. (Spring 1984). Faculty development and achievement: A faculty's view. *The Review of Higher Education, 7*(3), 205-222.

Brodkin, K. (1998). *How the Jews became white folks and what that says about race in America.* New Brunswick, NJ: Rutgers University Press.

Brophy, J.E. (1983). Research on the self-fulfilling prophecy and teacher expectation. *Journal of Educational Psychology, 75*(5), 631-661.

Butler, J., & Walter, J. (1991). Praxis and the prospect of curriculum transformation. In J. Butler & J. Walter (Eds.), *Transforming the curriculum: Ethnic studies and women's studies.* Albany, NY: State University of New York.

Buttery, T.J., Haberman, M., & Houston, W.R. (1990, Summer). First annual ATE survey of critical issues in teacher education. *Action in Teacher Education, 12*(2), 1-7.

Cadzen, C., & John, V.P. (1971). Learning in American Indian children. In M.L. Wax, S. Diamond, & F.O. Gearing (Eds.), *Anthropological perspectives on education.* New York: Basic Books.

Cadzen, C., & Leggett, E. (1981). Culturally responsive education recommendations for achieving Lau Remedies II*. In H. Trueba, G. Guthrie, & K. Au (Eds.), *Culture and the bilingual classroom studies in classroom ethnography.* Rowley, MA: Newbury House Publishers.

Carter, D. J., & Wilson, R. (1992). *Minorities in higher education: 1991 tenth annual status report.* Washington, D.C.: American Council on Education.

Caswell, H., & Campbell, D.S. (1935). *Curriculum development.* New York: American Book Company.

Centra, J.A. (1978). Types of faculty development programs. *Journal of Higher Education, 52*(4), 369-377.

Chace, W.M. (1990). The real challenge of multiculturalism (is yet to come). *Academe* (November/December), 20-23.

Chang, M., Witt-Sandis, D., & Hakuta, K. (1999, September). The dynamics of race in higher education: An examination of the evidence. *Equity & Excellence in Education, 32*, 12-16.

Chesler, M. (1996). *Resistance to the multicultural agenda in higher education.* (Working Paper No. 50). University of Michigan: The Program on Conflict Management Alternatives of the University of Michigan.

Chesler, M., & Crowfoot, J. (1989). *Racism in higher education I: An organizational analysis* (Working Paper No. 21). University of Michigan: The Program on Conflict Management Alternatives of the University of Michigan.

Chesler, M., & Crowfoot, J. (1997). *Racism in higher education II: Challenging racism and promoting multiculturalism in higher education organizations.* (Working Paper No. 558). University of Michigan: The Center for Research on Social Organization.

Churchill, W. (1992). *Fantasies of the master race: Literature, cinema and the colonization of American Indians.* (M.A. Jaimes, Ed.). Monroe, ME: Common Courage Press.

Clark, B.R., & Neave, G.R. (Eds.) (1992). *The encyclopedia of higher education,* Vol. 3, *Analytical perspectives.* New York: Pergamon Press.

Clark, S.M., Corcoran, M., & Lewis, D.R. (1986). The case for institutional perspective on faculty development. *Journal of Higher Education, 57*(2), 176-195.

Collett, J. & Serrano, B. (1992). Stirring it up: The inclusive classroom. In D. Schoem, L. Frankel, X. Zúñiga, & E. Lewis (Eds.), *Multicultural teaching in the university.* Westport, CT: Praeger.

Collins, P.H., & Andersen, M. (1988). *The inclusive curriculum: Race, class, and gender.* Washington, D.C.: American Sociological Association.

Corcoran, M., & Clark, S.M. (1984). Professional socialization and contemporary career attitudes of three faculty generations. *Research in Higher Education, 20*(2), 131-153.

Crow, K. (1997). Integrating trans-cultural knowledge into nursing curricula: An American Indian example. In A. Morey & M. Kitano (Eds.). *Multicultural course transformation in higher education.* Boston, MA: Allyn and Bacon Publishers.

Cueto, G., & Aaronshon, E. (1997). Moving within the monolith: The struggle to make a university culturally responsible. In C. Grant (Ed.), *Proceedings of the National Association for Multicultural Education: Seventh Annual NAME Conference* (pp. 291-296). Mahwah, NJ: Lawrence Erlbaum.

Cytrynbaum, S., Lee, S., & Wadner, D. (1982). Faculty development through the life course: Application of recent adult development theory and research. *Journal of Instructional Development, 5*(2), 11-22.

Daft, R. L. (1995). *Organization and theory and design.* San Francisco, CA: West Publishing Company.

Dale, E. (1998). *An assessment of a faculty development program at a research university.* Unpublished doctoral dissertation, University of Massachusetts Amherst.

Darder, A. (1995). Buscando America: The contribution of critical Latino educators to the academic development and empowerment of Latino students in the U.S. In C. Sleeter & P. McLaren (Eds.), *Multicultural education, critical pedagogy and the politics of difference.* Albany, NY: State University of New York.

Dean, T. (1989). Multicultural classrooms, monocultural teachers. *College Composition and Communication, 40*, 23-37.

Delpit, L. (1995). *Other people's children: Cultural conflict in the classroom.* New York: The New Press.

Dewey, J. (1900). *The school in society and the child and the curriculum.* Chicago, IL: University of Chicago Press.

Diaz, C. (Ed.). (1992). *Multicultural education for the 21st century.* Washington, D.C.: National Educational Association.

Dixon, V.J. (1997). The relationship between the cultural awareness of teachers and the frequency of behavior referrals among middle school males. In C. Grant (Ed.), *Proceedings of the National Association for Multicultural Education: Seventh Annual NAME Conference* (pp. 69-82). Mahwah, NJ: Lawrence Erlbaum.

Donath, J. (1997). The humanities. In A. Morey & M. Kitano (Eds.). *Multicultural course transformation in higher education.* Boston, MA: Allyn and Bacon Publishers.

Doppler, J. (2000). *A description of gay/straight alliances in the public schools of Massachusetts.* Unpublished doctoral dissertation, University of Massachusetts Amherst.

D'Souza, D. (1991). *Illiberal education: The politics of race and sex on campus.* New York: Vintage.

DuBois, W.E.B. (1935). *Black reconstruction.* New York: Harcourt, Brace.

Eaves, R. (1975). Teacher race, student race, and the behavior problem checklist. *Journal of Abnormal Child Psychology, 3*(1), 1-9.

Ebel, K.E., & McKeachie, W.J. (1985). *Improving undergraduate education through faculty development: An analysis of effective programs and practices.* San Francisco: Jossey-Bass.

Eisner, E.W. (1990). Creative curriculum development and practice. *Journal of Curriculum & Supervision, 6*(1), 62-73.

Eliot, J. (1985). Redefining women's education. In M. Schuster & S. Van Dyne (Eds.), *Women's place in the academy: Transforming the liberal arts curriculum.* New Jersey: Rowman & Allanheld.

Ellsworth, E. (1989). Why doesn't this feel empowering? In C. Luke and J. Gore (Eds.), *Feminism and Critical Pedagogy* (pp. 120-137). New York: Routledge.

Erickson, F. (1990, Spring). Culture, politics, and educational practice. *Educational Foundations*, 21-45.

Escueta, E., & O'Brien, E. (1995). Asian Americans in higher education. In D. T. Nakanishi & T. Y. Nishida (Eds.), The Asian American educational experience: A source book for teachers and students (pp. 259-272). New York: Routledge. (Original work published 1991).

Evans, C.C. (1995, June). *Faculty reflections on designing and implementing multicultural curricula: A transformative process.* Unpublished Dissertation. University of Minnesota.

Faderman, L. (1991). *Odd girls and twilight lovers: A history of lesbian life in twentieth-century America.* New York: Penguin.

Faderman, L. (1999). *To believe in women: What lesbians have done for America — a history.* Boston: Houghton Mifflin.

Feagin, J.R., Imani, N., & Vera, H. (1996). *The agony of education.* New York: Routledge.

Fordham, S., & Ogbu, J. (1986). Black students' school success: Coping with the burden of acting white. Urban Review, 18 (3), 176-206.

Foster, M. (1995). African American teachers and culturally relevant pedagogy. In J. Banks (Ed.), *Handbook of research on multicultural education.* New York: Macmillan.

Foster, M. (1997). *Black teachers on teaching.* New York: New York Press.

Freire, P. (1970). *Pedagogy of the oppressed.* New York: Seabury Press.

Friedman, E.G., Kolmar, W.K., Flint, C.B., & Rothenberg, P. (Eds.).(1996). *Creating an inclusive college curriculum.* New York: Columbia Teachers College.

Gaff, J. (1975). *Toward faculty renewal.* San Francisco, CA: Jossey-Bass.

Gall, M., Borg, W., & Gall, J. (1996). *Educational research: An introduction.* New York: Longman Publishers.

Garlikov, R. (June 11, 2000). Socratic Method: Teaching by asking instead of telling on-line]. http://www.garlikov.com/Soc_Meth.html

Gay, G. (1992). Effective teaching practices for multicultural classrooms. In C. Diaz (Ed.), *Multicultural education for the twenty-first century.* Washington, D.C.: National Education Association.

Gay, G. (1994). *A synthesis of scholarship in multicultural education.* Urban Monograph Series. Oak Brook, IL: NCREL.

Gay, G. (1995). Curriculum theory and multicultural education. In J. Banks & C. Banks (Eds.), *Handbook of research on multicultural education.* London: Macmillan.

Gay, G. (1997). Multicultural infusion in teacher education: Foundations and applications. *Peabody Journal of Education, 72*(1), 150-177.

Goodlad, J. (1983). A place called school. New York: McGraw Hill.

Goodwin, A.L., Genishi, C., Asher, N., and Woo, K. (1995). Asian American voices: Speaking out on the teaching profession. Paper presented at the annual meeting of the American Educational Research Association, San Francisco, CA.

Gore, J. (1993). A struggle for pedagogies. New York: Routledge.

Grant, C. (1994, Winter). Challenging the myths. The Newsletter of the National Association for Multicultural Education, 1(2), 4-8.

Green, M. (Ed.). (1989). *Minorities on campus: A handbook for enhancing diversity.* Washington, D.C.: American Council on Education.

Gurin, P. (1999, September). Selections from: The compelling need for diversity in higher education, expert reports in defense of the University of Michigan. *Equity & Excellence in Education, 32,* 36-62.

Guskey, T. (1988). *Improving student learning in college classrooms.* Springfield, IL: Charles C. Thomas.

Hale-Benson, J.E. (1986). Black children: Their roots, culture, and learning styles. Baltimore: The John Hopkins University Press.

Hammock, J., & Wilds, D. (2000, June 9). 17th Annual Status Report Press Release: Students of color continue to make modest gains in higher education enrollment and degree attainment, ACE study shows. *American Council on Education News (ACEnet)*. http://www.acenet.edu (2000, March 1).

Hardiman, R., & Jackson, B. (1992). Racial identity development: Understanding racial dynamics in college classrooms and on campus. In M. Adams (Ed.), *Promoting diversity in college classrooms: Innovative responses for the curriculum, faculty, and institutions.* (pp. 21-37). San Francisco, CA: Jossey-Bass.

Hardiman, R., & Jackson, B. (1994). Perspectives on race. In M. Adams, P. Brigham, P. Dalpes, and L Marchesani (Eds.), *Social diversity and social justice.* Dubuque, IA: Kendal/Hunt Publishing. (Original work published 1980).

Hasslen, R.C. (1993). *The effects of teaching strategies in multicultural education on monocultural students' perceptions.* Unpublished Dissertation, University of Minnesota.

Hays, W.L. (1994). *Statistics* (5th ed.). Fort Worth: Harcourt Brace.

Henry, A. (1993-4, Winter). There are no safe places: Pedagogy as powerful and dangerous terrain. *Action In Teacher Education, 15*(4), 1-4.

Hodgkinson, H. (1991). Reform versus reality. *Phi Delta Kappan, 73*(1), 9-16.

hooks, b. (1994). *Teaching to transgress.* New York: Routledge.

hooks, b. (1993). Transformative pedagogy and multiculturalism. In T. Perry & J. Fraser (Eds.), *Freedom's plow: Reaching in the multicultural classroom* (pp. 91-97). New York: Routledge.

Huber, T. (1991, October). *Restructuring to reclaim youth at risk: Culturally responsible pedagogy.* Paper presented at the 13th Annual Meeting of the Midwestern Educational Research Association, Chicago, IL.

Hunt, J., Bell, L.A., Wei, W., & Ingle, G. (1992, Winter). Monoculturalism to multiculturalism: Lessons from three public universities. In M. Adams (Ed.), *Promoting diversity in college classrooms: Innovative responses for the curriculum, faculty, and institutions.* San Francisco, CA: Jossey-Bass.

Irvine, J. (1992). Making teacher education culturally responsive. In M. Dilworth (Ed.), *Diversity in teacher education.* San Francisco, CA: Jossey-Bass.

Jackson, B., & Hardiman, R. (1994). Multicultural organizational development. In E. Cross, J. Katz, F. Miller, & E.W. Seashore (Eds.), *The promise of diversity: Over 40 voices discuss strategies for eliminating discrimination in organizations.* New York: Irwin.

Jackson, B., & Holvino, E. (1988). Developing multicultural organizations. *Creative Change: Journal of Religion and the Applied Behavioral Sciences, 9*(2), 14-19.

Jacob, E., Johnson, B., Finley, J., Gurski, J., & Lavine, R. (1996). One student at a time: The cultural inquiry process. *Middle School Journal, 27*(4), 29-34.

Jennings, K. (1994). *Becoming visible.* Boston, MA: Alyson Publications.

Jordan, C. (1985). Translating culture: From ethnographic information to educational program. *Anthropology and Education Quarterly, 16*, 105-123.

Joyce, B., & Weil, M. (1986). *Models of teaching* (3rd ed.). New Jersey: Prentice-Hall.

Kalantzis, M., Cope, B., & Slade, D. (1989). *Minority languages and dominant cultures: Issues of education, assessment and social equity.* New York: Falmer Press.

Katz, D., & Kahn, R. (1978). *The social psychology of organizations.* New York: Wiley.

Kindsvatter, R., Wilen, W., & Ishler, M. (1996). *Dynamics of effective teaching* (3rd ed.). New York: Longman.

Kitano, M. (1997a). A rationale and framework for course change. In Morey, A. & Kitano, M.(Eds.). *Multicultural course transformation in higher education.* Boston, MA: Allyn and Bacon Publishers.

Kitano, M. (1997b). What a course will look like after multicultural change. In A. Morey & M. Kitano (Eds.). *Multicultural course transformation in higher education.* Boston, MA: Allyn and Bacon Publishers.

Kivel, P. (1996). *Uprooting racism: How white people can work for racial justice.* Philadelphia, PA: New Society Publishers.

Kohl, H. (1995, September). I won't learn from you!: Confronting student resistance. *Rethinking Schools; Rethinking our Classrooms Special Edition* (2nd ed.), 134-135. (Original work published 1994).

Ladson-Billings, G. (1994). *The Dreamkeepers.* San Francisco: Jossey-Bass.

List, K. (1997). A continuing conversation on teaching: An evaluation of a decade-long Lilly Teaching Fellows Program 1986-1996. *To Improve the Academy, 16,* 201-224.

Lowman, J. (1995). *Mastering the techniques of teaching.* San Francisco, CA: Jossey-Bass.

Maher, F., & Tetreault, M. (1992). Inside feminist classrooms: An ethnographic approach. *New Directions for Teaching and Learning, 49,* 57-74.

Marchesani, L., & Adams, M. (1992). Dynamics of diversity in the teaching-learning process: A faculty development model for analysis and action. In M. Adams (Ed.), *Promoting diversity in college classrooms: Innovative responses for the curriculum, faculty, and institutions* (pp. 9-20). San Francisco, CA: Jossey-Bass.

Marshall, C., & Rossman, G. (1999). *Designing Qualitative Research* (3rd ed.). Thousand Oaks, CA: Sage.

Mayberry, K. J. (1996). *Teaching what you're not: Identity politics in higher education.* New York: New York University Press.

McKeachie, W. J. (1965). *Teaching tips: A guide-book for the beginning college teacher.* Ann Arbor, MI: G. Wahr.

McKinney, D. C. (1998). *Not behind a podium: A qualitative study of self-defined practitioners of empowering pedagogy in postsecondary teaching (faculty).* Unpublished Dissertation, University of Georgia.

Mellander, G.A. (1998). College-bound Hispanics. *The Hispanic Outlook in Higher Education, 8*(12), 4.

Menges, Mathis, Haliburton, Marincovich & Svinicki. (1988). Morey, A. & Kitano, M. (Eds.) (1997). *Multicultural course transformation in higher education.* Boston, MA: Allyn and Bacon Publishers.

Merian, L. (1928). *The problem of Indian administration.* Baltimore, MD: Johns Hopkins Press.

Meyers, J. L., & Wells, A. D. (1995). *Research design and statistical analysis*. Hillsdale, NJ: Erlbaum.

Midwest Higher Education Commission. (1995). *Minority faculty development report*. Minneapolis, MN: MHEC.

Milem, J.F. (1999, January). *The Importance of faculty diversity to student learning and to the mission of higher education*. Paper-in-progress presented at the American Council on Education's Research Symposium and Working Meeting on Affirmative Action, Arlington, VA.

Mohatt, G., & Erickson, F. (1981). Cultural differences in teaching styles in an Odawa school: A sociolinguistic approach. In H. Trueba, G. Guthrie, & K. Au (Eds.), *Culture and the bilingual classroom studies in classroom ethnography*. Rowley, MA: Newbury House Publishers.

Moore, W.L., & Cooper, H. (1984). Correlations between teacher and student background and teacher perceptions of disciplinary techniques. *Psychology in the Schools, 21*, 386-392.

Moran, K. (1996, August). *Teaching behaviors and Teacher values that contribute to effective multicultural and gender-inclusive education: A qualitative study*. Unpublished Dissertation. University of Massachusetts Amherst.

Murray, R. K. (1993, June). *Freireian pedagogy in a college classroom: An action research project (basic skills, pedagogy)*. Unpublished Dissertation, University of New York at Buffalo.

Musil, C.M., Garcia, M., Moses, Y. & Smith, D.G. (1995). *Diversity in higher education: A work in progress*. Washington, D.C.: Association of American Colleges and Universities.

NCES Enrollment in Higher Education: Fall 1995 (1997, May). *National Center for Educational Statistics*. http://nces.ed.giv/pubs97/97440.html (2000, June 9).

NCES Fast Facts: Enrollment. *National Center for Educational Statistics.* (1999, August 9), Amherst, MA.

NCES Fast Facts: Enrollment. *National Center for Educational Statistics.* <http://www.nces.ed.gov/display.asp?id = 18> (2000, June 9).

NCES Fast Facts: Race/ethnicity of postsecondary faculty. *National Center for Educational Statistics*, U.S. Department of Education, Instructional Faculty and Staff in Higher Education Institutions: Fall 1987 and Fall 1992. (1997). http://nces.ed.gov.fastfacts/display.asp?id = 61 (2000, June 9).

Nieto, S. (1999). *The light in their eyes: Creating multicultural learning communities*. New York: Teachers College Press.

Nieto, S. (2000). *Affirming diversity: The sociopolitical context of multicultural education* (3rd ed.). New York: Longman.

Obear, K. (1993, July). *What is a multicultural campus?* Paper presented at the ACUHO-I College Conference on the Multicultural Campus: Creating Organizational Change. Amherst, MA.

Ortega, R., José, C., Zúñiga, X., & Gutierrez, L. (1993). Latinos in the United States: A framework for teaching. In D. Schoem, L. Frankel, X. Zúñiga, & E. Lewis (Eds.), *Multicultural teaching in the university*. Westport, CT: Praeger.

Osborne, B. (1991). Towards an ethnology of culturally responsive pedagogy in small-scale remote communities: Native American and Torres Strait Islander. *Qualitative Studies in Education, 4*(1), 1-17.

Ouellet, M., & Sorcinelli, M. (1995). Teaching and learning in the diverse classroom: A faculty and TA partnership program. *To Improve the Academy, 14*, 205-217.

Ouellet, M. & Sorcinelli, M. (1998). TA training: Strategies for responding to diversity in the classroom. In M. Marincovich, J. Prostko, F. Stout (Eds.), *The professional development of graduate teaching assistants* (pp. 105-120). Boston, MA: Anker.

Ouellet, M., & Stanley, C. (1997-1998). Instructional technology and diversity: Parallel challenges for our institutions. In *Journal of Staff, Program, & Organization Development, 15*(1), 5-10.

Ouellet, M., & Stanley, C. (2000). On the path: POD as a multicultural organization. In M. Kaplan (Ed.), *To Improve the Academy, 18*, 38-54.

Paccione, A., & McWhorter, B. (1997). Multicultural Perspective Transformation of teachers: The impact of cultural immersion. In C. Grant (Ed.), *Proceedings of the National Association for Multicultural Education: Seventh Annual NAME Conference* (pp.479-500). Mahwah, NJ: Lawrence Erlbaum.

Patton, M.Q. (1990). Qualitative evaluation and research methods. (2nd Ed.). Newbury Park, CA: Sage Publications.

Philips, A, (1973). Participation structures and communicative competence: Warm Springs children in community and classroom. In C.B. Cadzen, V.P. John, & D. Hymes (Eds.), *Functions of language in the classroom*. New York: Teachers College.

Presidents Initiative on Race website, one America. (1999, April). www.whitehouse.gov/Initiatives.

Rakow, L. (1991, Summer). Gender and race in the classroom: Teaching way out of line. *Feminist Teacher, 6*(1), 10-13.

Reed, D.F. (1993). Multicultural education for preservice students. *Action in Teacher Education, 15*(3), 27-34.

Rhoades, G. (1991, Summer). Dealing with racism in the classroom. *Feminist Teacher, 6*(1), 34-36.

Romney Associates, Inc. (2000). *Cultural competence* [handout]. Amherst, MA

Rose, P. (1974). *They and we: Racial and ethnic relations in the United States* (2nd ed.). New York: Random House.

Rosensitto, A. (1999). *Faculty Perceptions of the Need for Graduate Programs to Included Formal Curricula Design to Prepare Candidates to teach in College and University Settings.* Unpublished doctoral dissertation, Pepperdine University.

Rosenthal, J. W. (1997). Multicultural science: Focus on the biological and environmental sciences. In A. Morey & M. Kitano (Eds.). *Multicultural course transformation in higher education*. Boston, MA: Allyn and Bacon Publishers.

Rothenberg, P. (1996). Transforming the curriculum: The New Jersey Project experience. In E. Friedman, W. Kolmar, C. Flint, & P. Rothenberg (Eds.). *Creating an inclusive college classroom*. New York: Teachers College.

Rubino, A.N. (1994). *Faculty development programs and evaluation in American colleges and universities.* Unpublished doctoral dissertation, Western Michigan University.

Sarracent, M.C. (2000, April 7). The Ivy League review: Part one. *The Hispanic Outlook in Higher Education, 10* (14), 10-11.

Saulter, L.H. (1996). *Teacher's attitudes toward multicultural education.* Unpublished Dissertation, North Carolina State University.

Schlesinger, M. A. Jr., (1998). *The disuniting of America: Reflection on a multicultural society.* New York: Norton.

Schmitz, B. (1992). Cultural pluralism and core curricula. In M. Adams (Ed.), *Promoting diversity in college classrooms: Innovative responses for the curriculum, faculty, and institutions* (pp. 61-70). San Francisco, CA: Jossey-Bass.

Schoem, D., Frankel, L., Zúñiga, X., Lewis, E. (1995). The meaning of multiculturalism. In D. Schoem, L. Frankel, X. Zúñiga, & E. Lewis (Eds.). *Multicultural teaching in the University* (p. 1-12). Westport, CT: Praeger.

Schultz, A. (1992). *On the road to multiculturalism: A PCMA seminar report* (Working Paper No. 33). University of Michigan: The Program on Conflict Management Alternatives of the University of Michigan.

Schuster, M., & Van Dyne, S. (1985a). Curricular change for the twenty-first century: Why women? In M. Schuster & S. Van Dyne (Eds.), *Women's place in the academy: Transforming the liberal arts curriculum.* New Jersey: Rowman & Allanheld.

Schuster, M., & Van Dyne, S. (1985b). Stages of curriculum transformation. In M. Schuster & S. Van Dyne (Eds.), *Women's place in the academy: Transforming the liberal arts curriculum.* New Jersey: Rowman & Allanheld.

Schuster, M., & Van Dyne, S. (1985c). The changing classroom. In M. Schuster & S. Van Dyne (Eds.), *Women's place in the academy: Transforming the liberal arts curriculum.* New Jersey: Rowman & Allanheld.

Sfeir-Younis, L. (1995). Reflections on the teaching of multicultural courses. In D. Schoem, L. Frankel, X. Zúñiga, & E. Lewis (Eds.), *Multicultural teaching in the university.* Westport, CT: Praeger.

Sheets, R.H., & Gay, G. (1996). Student perceptions of disciplinary conflict in ethnically diverse classrooms. *National Association of Secondary School Principles, 80*(580), 84-94.

Shewsbury, C. (1997). What is feminist pedagogy? *Women's Studies Quarterly 1 & 2,* 166-173.

Shor, I. (1987). Educating the educators: A Freirean approach to the crisis in teacher education. In I. Shor (Ed.)., *Freire for the classroom: A sourcebook for liberatory teaching.* Portsmouth, NH: Boyton/Cook.

Shor, I. (1992). *Empowering education: Critical teaching for social change.* Chicago: University of Chicago Press.

Shor, I., & Freire, P. (1987). The dream of liberating education. In I. Shor & P. Freire (Eds.). *A pedagogy for liberation: Dialogues on transforming education.* New York: Bergin & Garvey.

Shujaa, M. J. (1992). Education and schooling: You can have one without the other. In M. J. Shujaa, (Ed.), *Too little education* (pp. 13-36). Trenton, NJ: Africa World Press.

Skutnabb-Kangas, T. (1990). Legitimating or delegitimating new forms of racism: The role of researchers. *Journal of Multilingual and Multicultural Development, 11*(1 & 2), 77-100.

Sleeter, C. (1992, Spring). Resisting racial awareness: How teachers understand the social order from their racial, gender, and social class locations. *Educational Foundations, 6*(2), 7-32.

Sleeter, C. & Grant, C. (1987, November). An analysis of multicultural education in the United States. *Harvard Educational Review, 57*(4), 421-444.

Smith, D., & Schonfeld, N. (2000, November). The benefits of diversity: What the research tells us. *About Campus,* 16-23.

Smith, D.G., Gerbick, G.L., Figueroa, M.A., Watkins, G.H., Levitan, T., et al (1997). *Diversity works: The emerging picture of how students benefit.* Washington, D.C.: Association of American Colleges & Universities.

Spring, J. (1997). *Deculturalization and the struggle for equality.* New York: McGraw-Hill.

Spring, J. (2000). *The intersection of cultures: Multicultural education in the United States and the Global Economy* (2nd ed.). Boston: McGraw Hill.

Steele, S. (1989, February). **The recoloring of campus life; student racism, academic pluralism, and the end of a dream.** *Harper's Magazine, 278*(1665), 47(9).

Stodolsky, S.S., & Leser, G.S. (1967, Fall). Learning patterns in the disadvantaged. *Harvard Educational Review, 31,* 546-593.

Suzuki, B. (1979). Multicultural education: What's it all about? *Integrated Education, 17*(97-98), 43-50.

Tharp, R., Jordan, C., & O'Donnell, C. (1980). *Behavioral community psychology: A cross disciplinary example with theoretical implications.* Paper presented at the annual meeting of the American Psychological Association, Montreal.

Thenlin, J. (1990). *The American college and university: A history.* Athens, GA: University of Georgia.

Thomas, M.D. (1982, Winter). The limits of pluralism. *The Newsletter for the National Association for Multicultural Education 1*(2), 589-592.

University of Massachusetts Amherst Office of the Chancellor. (1997-2001). *Strategic Action Plan.* (October 2000), Amherst, MA.

University of Massachusetts Amherst Office of Institutional Research (OIR). (1998-2000). *Factbook.* Amherst, MA.

University of Massachusetts Amherst Office of Institutional Research (OIR). (2000-2001). UMass at a glance [Brochure]. Amherst, MA.

University of Massachusetts Amherst Office of Institutional Research (OIR). (2001, October 15). Factbook Update: Race/ethnicity and gender of staff by job classification. Fall 1994-Fall 2000. <<http://www.umass.edu/oapa>> (2001, August 10).

Valverde, L. (1981). Achieving equity in higher education: Inclusion and retention of Hispanic academics. In T.H. Escobedo (Ed.), *Education and Chicanos: Issues and research.* Los Angeles, CA: Spanish Speaking Mental Health Research Center.

Valverde, L. (1998). Future strategies and actions: Creating multicultural higher education campuses. In L. Valverde & L. Castenell, Jr. (Eds.), *The multicultural campus: Strategies for transforming higher education*. London: Altamira.

Virtualology: Rhetorical Theory (VRT). (2000, July 4). Socratic method definition and links to resources. <<http://www.socracticmethod.net>> (2001, December 1).

Vogt, L., Jordan, C., & Tharp, R. (1987). Explaining school failure, producing school success: Two cases. *Anthropology and Education Quarterly, 18,* 276-286.

Wax, M., Wax, R., & Dumont, R. (1974). *Formal education in an American Indian community*. Kalamazoo, MI: The Society of the Study of Social Problems.

Weiler, K. (1988). *Women teaching for change: Gender, class & power*. New York: Bergin & Garvey Publishers.

Wellman, D. (1977). *Portraits of white racism*. Cambridge, England: Cambridge University Press.

West, C. (1994). *Race Matters*. New York: Vintage.

WICHE: Western Interstate Commission for Higher Education. (1991). *The road to college: Educational progress by race and ethnicity*. Boulder, CO: Western Interstate Commission for Higher Education.

Wijeyesinghe, C., Griffin, P., and Love, B. Racism curriculum design. In M. Adams, L.A. Bell, & P. Griffin (Eds.), *Teaching for diversity and social justice: A sourcebook*. New York: Routledge.

Wilds, D., & Wilson, R. (1999, December). 16th Annual Status Report News Release From the American Council on Education's Office of Minorities in Higher Education. *American Council on Education news (ACEnet)*. <http://www.acenet.edu> (January 1, 2000).

Wiles, J., & Bondi, J. (1993). *Curriculum development: A guide to practice* (3rd ed.). New York: Maxwell Macmillan International.

Williams, G.W. (1882-1883). *History of the Negro race in America from 1619 to 1880: Negroes as slaves, as soldiers, and as citizens* (2 vols.). New York: G.P. Putman's Sons.

Wlodkowski, R., & Ginsberg, M. (1995). *Diversity and motivation: Culturally responsive teaching*. San Francisco, CA: Jossey-Bass.

Woodson, C.G. (1933). *The mis-education of the Negro*. Washington, D.C.: The Associated Publishers.

Wright, B. (1995, Summer). The broken covenant: American Indian missions in the colonial colleges. *Tribal College, 7*(1), 26-33.

Wyngaard, M.A.V. (1998, December). *Stakeholders visions of culturally relevant education in an urban high school community*. Unpublished doctoral dissertation. Kent State University, OH.

Zinn, H. (1980). The people's history of the United States. New York: HarperCollins.

Zintz, M. (1969). *Education across cultures*. Iowa: Kendal/Hunt Publishing.

Index